P9-DOD-949

THE BEDFORD SERIES IN HISTORY AND CULTURE

Plunkitt of Tammany Hall

A Series of Very Plain Talks
on Very Practical Politics

THE BEDFORD SERIES IN HISTORY AND CULTURE
Advisory Editors: Natalie Zemon Davis and Ernest R. May

THE BEDFORD SERIES IN HISTORY AND CULTURE

Plunkitt
of Tammany Hall

A Series of Very Plain Talks
on Very Practical Politics

BY WILLIAM L. RIORDON

Edited with an introduction by

Terrence J. McDonald

University of Michigan

BEDFORD BOOKS   Boston ≈ New York

For Bedford Books

President and Publisher: Charles H. Christensen
Associate Publisher/General Manager: Joan E. Feinberg
History Editor: Sabra Scribner
Associate History Editor: Louise D. Townsend
Managing Editor: Elizabeth M. Schaaf
Copyeditor: Barbara G. Flanagan
Text Design: Claire Seng-Niemoeller
Cover Design: Richard Emery Design
Cover Art: Detail from a photograph of George W. Plunkitt. Euphemia Vale Blake. *History of The Tammany Society or Columbian Order from Its Organization to the Present Time.* New York: Souvenir Publishing Company, 1901, p. 202. Courtesy of the Harvard College Library.

Library of Congress Catalog Card Number: 92-77721

Copyright © 1994 by Bedford Books
A Division of St. Martin's Press, Inc.

All rights reserved. No part of this book may be reproduced, stored in a retrieval system, or transmitted by any form or by any means, electronic, mechanical, photocopying, recording, or otherwise, except as may be expressly permitted by the applicable copyright statutes or in writing by the Publisher.

Manufactured in the United States of America.

8

f   e

For information, write: Bedford Books, 75 Arlington Street, Boston MA 02116
(617–426–7440)

ISBN: 0-312-08444-7 (paperback)
ISBN: 0-312-09666-6 (hardcover)

Acknowledgments

Pages 9, 19, 30: Courtesy of the Edwin P. Kilroe Collection, Rare Book and Manuscript Library, Columbia University.
Page 26: Courtesy of the General Library, Columbia University.
Pages 109–110: Courtesy of the Oral History Related Papers, Rare Book and Manuscript Library, Columbia University.

Foreword

The *Bedford Series in History and Culture* is designed so that readers can study history as historians do.

The historian's first task is finding the evidence. Documents, letters, memoirs, interviews, pictures, movies, novels, or poems can provide facts and clues. Then the historian questions and compares the sources. There is more to do than in a courtroom, for hearsay evidence is welcome, and the historian is usually looking for answers beyond act and motive. Different views of an event may be as important as a single verdict. How a story is told may yield as much information as what it says.

Along the way the historian seeks help from other historians and perhaps from specialists in other disciplines. Finally, it is time to write, to decide on an interpretation and how to arrange the evidence for readers.

Each book in this series contains an important historical document or group of documents, each document a witness from the past and open to interpretation in different ways. The documents are combined with some element of historical narrative—an introduction or a biographical essay, for example—that provides students with an analysis of the primary source material an important background information about the world in which it was produced.

Each book in the series focuses on a specific topic within a specific historical period. Each provides a basis for lively thought and discussion about several aspects of the topic and the historian's role. Each is short enough (and inexpensive enough) to be a reasonable one-week assignment in a college course. Whether as classroom or personal reading, each book in the series provides firsthand experience of the challenge—and fun—of discovering, recreating and interpreting the past.

Natalie Zemon Davis
Ernest R. May

Preface

George Washington Plunkitt was a man of his times. Like many men who were born before the Civil War and came into political power in the late nineteenth century, Plunkitt owed his most important loyalties to his ethnic group and his political party. Convinced that the Irish were the supreme race, he thought nothing of using derogatory terms to refer to other ethnic groups. Believing that woman suffrage was "unamerican," he viewed politics as a "man's" world and thought that the measures of a successful politician were the size of his political following and the fortune he accumulated in and through politics. Education, oratory, and even political issues were all irrelevant to politics according to Plunkitt. For him the state was not a mechanism for solving social problems as much as a source of individualized benefits that he could distribute to his followers as part of his largess. He opposed civil service laws because they threatened his supply of jobs for his supporters, and he opposed the public supervision of primary elections because this made it harder for the machine to control political nominations.

In all of these attitudes Plunkitt was representative of many men of his times. Because he was, he did not see that the political ground beneath him was shifting even as he was discussing his political life and philosophy with William L. Riordon. Women and members of more recently arrived ethnic groups were striving for and achieving political power; commitment to a reform program was replacing party loyalty among many; and reform politicians (both within and outside of Tammany Hall) were developing a theory that saw the state as a source of social services available to all (mother's pensions, unemployment compensation, and so on) rather than of benefits to be handed out by politicians. Plunkitt was defeated in 1904, 1905, and 1907 by men who were better educated, better orators, and better able to mobilize voters around issues, in this case Plunkitt's own corruption. These defeats were deeply ironic given Plunkitt's attitudes as well as symptomatic of the direction of politics to come. The politicians of the next generation, too, would have their contradictions and blind spots, but they would be different from those of Plunkitt.

Plunkitt of Tammany Hall is, therefore, not a set of timeless maxims for practical politics but an invaluable record of public political views on the verge of oblivion. In fact, the power of the newer reform views is demonstrated by the portions of this book that respond to muckraker Lincoln Steffens's criticism of the "grafting" of machine politicians. Unknown to Plunkitt and other powers in Tammany Hall, the clock was ticking for the machine, too. Just twenty-five years after the publication of *Plunkitt of Tammany Hall,* the Tammany machine itself began to collapse under twin assaults from New York Mayor Fiorello La Guardia and the political mobilizations stirred up by Franklin Roosevelt's New Deal. The ignominious symbolic end came in 1943 when the Tammany headquarters building— newly built in 1929—had to be sold.

About one thing Plunkitt was absolutely right, however. Politics is hard work. In *The Shame of the Cities* Lincoln Steffens proposed somewhat blithely that "all we have to do is to establish a steady demand for good government." This is true, of course, but it radically underestimates the amount of energy and commitment necessary for political change. We do not get the politics we want; only the politics for which we are willing to work. American politics then and now requires both a broad social vision and a kind of relentless focus and energy. Plunkitt and the men like him are indeed a model of the latter.

Editing is also hard work, and a number of people have done their best to help turn my understanding of Plunkitt into something useful for others. Chuck Christensen, publisher of Bedford Books, first proposed this project to me, and he gave me much encouragement along the way. Series editor Ernest R. May of Harvard University gave me many good tips at an early point in the project. Bedford history editor Sabra Scribner and her assistant Louise Townsend did their best to keep me on track via a steady stream of phone calls and faxes containing both useful suggestions and helpful encouragement. Barbara Flanagan provided a thoroughgoing and very helpful copyediting and Elizabeth Schaaf, managing editor of Bedford's production department, had the thankless task of trying to keep this project on schedule against an author's dilatory instincts.

Reviewers of the manuscript of my introduction helped me to reformulate it in useful ways. For this I am very grateful to Steven J. Diner of George Mason University; Philip J. Ethington of the University of Southern California; Joanne Fraser; Timothy J. Gilfoyle of Loyola University, Chicago; Kenneth T. Jackson of Columbia University; Roger Lotchin of the University of North Carolina at Chapel Hill; and Judith Ann Trolander of the University of Minnesota at Duluth. Daniel Czitrom of Mount Holyoke College, Timothy Gilfoyle of Loyola University, David Hammack of Case Western Reserve University, and David Scobey of the University of Michigan all took time out of their busy schedules to share their New York expertise with me. Rudolf Ellenbogen and his staff at the Rare Book and Manuscript Library at Columbia University made research there a pleasure. The resources of the New-York Historical Society were also essential to this project as was the help of Mariam Touba, newspaper librarian at the Society.

My greatest debt, however, is to three graduate students who have worked with me on the project of which this consideration of Plunkitt is a part. The interest, energy, and enthusiasm of Stephen Frank, Victoria Getis, and Michael Smith have been precious gifts indeed.

Terrence J. McDonald

Contents

Introduction: How George Washington Plunkitt Became *Plunkitt of Tammany Hall*

Plunkitt of Tammany Hall is a contemporaneous portrayal of one of the best-known types of political organization in American history: the urban political machine. The years from about 1890 to 1910 were the heyday of the political machine, and in those days there was no machine more famous than Tammany Hall in New York City. George Washington Plunkitt, a well-known figure in New York politics from the 1860s until his death in 1924, was a district leader or "ward boss" in the Tammany Hall machine from about 1880 to 1905. Since its publication in 1905, *Plunkitt of Tammany Hall* has given generations of journalists, teachers, and students a passport into the world of controversy, conflict, corruption, and color that surrounded the political machines at their zenith. This book has thus influenced how we think of these organizations ever since.

1

Plunkitt of Tammany Hall is not simply an exact record of the words of Plunkitt, however; it is, rather, the product of a collaboration between a lifelong politician with a carefully crafted public image and a journalist seeking to write a book that would sell. Plunkitt wished to portray himself as powerful, wealthy, generous, and both loyal to and important in Tammany Hall. The book's editor, New York *Evening Post* reporter William L. Riordon, wanted a book that was both entertaining and timely. For Riordon's purposes it was useful to push Plunkitt's self-portrayals toward a sort of humorous extreme. Riordon also encouraged or perhaps even authored Plunkitt's widely quoted comments on "honest and dishonest graft" so that the book would be seen as a response to Lincoln Steffens's widely read book *The Shame of the Cities,* which was published the year before Plunkitt's.

This perhaps inevitably uneasy collaboration produced a book that is a mixture of stories capturing extraordinarily well the ambiguities of urban machine politics in America. Through *Plunkitt of Tammany Hall,* we see the generosity and selfishness, democracy and hierarchy, service and corruption that were the components of machine politics everywhere. Some readers of this book see Plunkitt as a lovable political pragmatist while others find in him a corrupt and self-serving windbag. As a successful machine politician, Plunkitt was by necessity a little bit of all of these things.

To understand why this is so—and thus get the most out of reading this book—we need to place *Plunkitt of Tammany Hall* carefully in its historical context by considering three related questions: First, what was a political machine and what role did a ward boss play in it? Second, who was George Washington Plunkitt and what did he stand for? And third, what were the circumstances in which this book first appeared? This introduction will offer some answers to these questions. In addition, Part Two, Related Materials, contains documents from Plunkitt's own times, some describing him, others expressing typical thinking about the political machine at the time. Use these resources to help find your own answers to these questions. You may discover things about this book or its times that no one else has.

POLITICAL STASIS IN TURBULENT TIMES: THE MACHINE AND THE STRUGGLE FOR POLITICAL CONTROL

George Washington Plunkitt was born in New York City on November 17, 1842, and he died there on November 19, 1924. His life spanned a period of immense and tumultuous social change in the United States. When Plunkitt was born, the American economy was primarily agricultural, its population was primarily rural, and mass immigration was just getting under way. When he died, the United States was the leading industrial power in the world, more than half the population lived in urban areas, and much of that population was foreign-born or first-generation American. Each of these major changes generated so much social conflict that the years from about 1877 to the turn of the twentieth century—the years when Plunkitt was at the peak of his political power—are known by historians today as the age of the "great upheaval." The rise of industrial capitalism created both new economic opportunities and new, more glaring forms of inequality. Mass immigration brought ambitious new citizens to the United States and raised controversial questions about how their differences in cultures and mores could be assimilated within the same national identity. The growth of great cities heightened and focused these problems. The sheer existence of the cities threatened the myth of the United States as a society of "sturdy yeoman farmers," while their physical forms were inscribed with the new social geography of difference and inequality and their streets were frequently the sites of the conflicts endemic to the age—strikes, ethnic violence, and the like.[1]

In an impressive—indeed moving—display of faith in the ballot box, the white male voters constituting the late-nineteenth-century electorate marched to the polls by the millions seeking political solutions to these issues. Would American society see increasing inequality or a more just distribution of the abundance the economy promised? Would the values and mores of the immigrants or the native-born be honored and legalized? What would the role of the government be in these matters? Immigrants and native-born, workers and farmers, members of a newly emergent middle class and leaders of corporate capital fought pitched political and ideological battles over these and other issues involving the future of American society. And those battles drove electoral participation to the highest levels in American history. But the paradoxical result of this activity seemed to be deadlock and business as usual.[2]

To some observers this deadlock was the result of the political parties themselves and so these years were also a time when honest men and women strenuously disagreed on the value of parties to American society. To their critics the parties had become corrupt large-scale bureaucracies fatally compromised by their relationships with business and more interested in holding and distributing government patronage—jobs and contracts—than in advocating any political principles. In this view the leadership of the parties placed electoral victory above all else because only that victory would bring both the patronage resources that held the parties together and the policymaking power that would permit them to reward their economically powerful backers. Therefore, party leaders minimized discussion of important issues, wrote platforms full of meaningless generalities, and then marched voters to the polls urging them to ignore the issues and vote on the basis of party loyalty. Once in office elected officials enriched themselves and the coffers of the parties by protecting the interests of the corporations that were their biggest financial backers. The defenders of the party system claimed, on the contrary, that it was precisely their organizing, mobilizing, and compromising efforts that held American democracy together. In their view high levels of voting occurred only because the parties were organized from the national level all the way down to the neighborhood voting precinct and therefore were able to get voters to the polls. Furthermore, party loyalty and platform compromises helped keep America from tearing itself apart along the economic and social divisions in the electorate. If supporters of the victorious party received jobs and contracts from the government, it was a small enough price to pay for a fully functioning democracy. And if, once in office, policymakers seemed to protect the interests of business, that was because economic development was good for all.[3]

This debate over the role of political parties had deep roots in American history (and has by no means been resolved even today), in part because parties were something of an unplanned afterthought in the American political system. In spite of their centrality in American politics, parties are not called for in the Constitution and did not even exist in anything like their contemporary form for the first thirty years or so after the Constitution was ratified in 1789. Parties were irrelevant to the Founding Fathers, who held to a sort of "amateur" theory of politics according to which men were called from their private affairs to take care of political business and then returned to their previous occupations. For them the ideal voter and officeholder were those willing to put their own interests aside and work for the broader good of the country. The idea of "professional" politicians who made their livings in and through politics would have horrified them. However, splits among the founders over political economy, constitutional interpretation, and foreign policy were institutionalized in party-like caucuses in Congress and the state legislatures during the first years after the ratification of the Constitution. As the states removed various barriers to universal white male suffrage in the early nineteenth century, the growing size of the electorate and the geographical expanse of the nation required more thoroughgoing organization for presidential elections, and in the 1820s and 1830s these party-like organizations began to act more like parties, funding newspapers, holding public caucuses and nomination conventions, and setting up their own internal organizations.[4]

As early as the presidential terms of Andrew Jackson (1828–1836), the parties began to support themselves by advocating the principle of "rotation in office," according to which appointed jobs at the various levels of government went to political supporters of the victorious party. This practice was christened the "spoils" system by one of Jackson's supporters who declared that he saw nothing wrong with the philosophy that "to the [political] victors belong the enemy's spoils of war." Throughout the rest of the nineteenth century most appointed government offices and contracts were distributed to supporters of the party in power. Furthermore, officeholders were usually expected to "contribute" some portion of their salaries (and holders of contracts some portion of their fees) to the party from which they received the patronage. In this way the spoils system—called more neutrally "patronage democracy"—both provided government employment for party supporters and financed some of the costs of the party's own employees and activities.[5]

As the century went on, the increasing scope, scale, and resources of corporations brought them into more contact with government and made them another source of funds for the parties. For example, as state legislatures chartered, invested in, regulated (or refused to regulate) railroads, the corporations found it useful to invest in the parties at the same time as politicians realized that they could enrich themselves and build their political campaign funds by charging corporations for their advice or votes. In this way the "spoils" of politics expanded beyond the jobs and contracts of government itself and into the private sector. As politicians became more dependent on these additions to their supplies of patronage it was not surprising that government policy became more protective of business interests.

Much of the contemporaneous discussion of the effects of this spoils system was focused on the American city because the cities and the parties had in effect grown up together. At the same time as the parties were emerging in the 1830s, the United States entered a hundred-year period of rapid urbanization based on the explosive population growth stimulated by immigration and industrialization. As the great metropolises like New York City grew, their political leadership faced formidable challenges as both party organizers and public policymakers. As politicians they needed to naturalize immigrants, register voters, and build political organizations, all the while attempting to exceed the same efforts of the other party. As elected policymakers the politicians were responsible for organizing the provision of government services and building local infrastructure. Most large cities introduced professional police and fire departments by the 1860s, began to build rudimentary school systems in the 1870s, and needed scores or even hundreds of clerks to transact routine business such as the sale of property or the conduct of elections. At the same time, cities contracted for other services: purchasing water, gas, and later electric light, offering franchises for the provision of public transportation, and letting contracts for the construction of streets, public buildings, harbors, and parks.[6]

For local politicians already familiar with patronage in national politics, it seemed perfectly natural to use local patronage to build municipal political organizations. And in the larger cities there was a good deal of patronage to use. In New York City in the 1880s, for example, the victorious political party controlled about twelve thousand jobs on the public payroll and influenced about twice as many more on municipally franchised or contracted projects. Meanwhile the "contributions" to the party of those holding the jobs or contracts provided a large war chest of funds for conducting further political activities. The key to using this patronage for the political advantage of one party or individual was organization and political control. Politicians ambitious to lead organizations that controlled entire cities had to mobilize enough voters to elect the number of city legislators (e.g., councilmen, aldermen, etc.) necessary to control the making of city policy, especially the awarding of jobs and contracts. The urban political machines were simply the local political organizations that achieved this control, and their leaders were known as "bosses."[7]

Aspiring bosses frequently began their careers by securing control of their own wards and thus becoming "ward bosses" because city legislators were usually elected by wards. Often a would-be ward boss made his first run for office on the basis of popularity he achieved in other all-male activities, like neighborhood gangs or volunteer fire companies. Once in office, ward bosses tried to maintain their power by constructing a ward-level organization that recruited enough voters to elect them and the candidates they supported. Ward bosses usually appointed representatives—called precinct or election district captains—to work on their behalf at the block or neighborhood level. Together the boss and these assistants offered rewards and services to those who voted their way. The most prized reward was a patronage job or contract, of course, and the best of these went to the precinct captains themselves. Ward leaders also hosted neighborhood outings and athletic events, sponsored a variety of political and other organizations in the ward, and offered voters some help finding employment in the private sector and dealing with municipal bureaucracies or courts. The bosses—or more likely the precinct captains—sometimes also offered voters small loans or gifts of cash, food, or fuel, including the almost proverbial holiday turkey or wintertime bucket of coal.[8]

For those bosses who succeeded at the ward level of politics, the road to citywide power offered yet another set of challenges. At the city level the relevant actors were other ward leaders just as ambitious and strategically skillful, and the goal was to build a coalition of ward bosses who would agree on one of themselves as the boss of the citywide organization. This boss would direct the efforts of the organization's members in the city legislature and allocate the patronage among the other ward bosses. The process of building a citywide organization with strong roots among the voters and control of the city's policymaking apparatus was slow, painstaking, and only rarely completed. Between 1870 and 1945 most—but not all—of the largest American cities were controlled to some extent by political machines, but machines that controlled entire cities—like Tammany Hall—were both rare and short-lived. The most common form of political machine was based in one or a few wards at most. The limits on machine building were to a great extent built into the system of patronage democracy.[9]

The first of these limits, ironically, was the supply of patronage resources itself, which was far from infinite. The forty thousand jobs influenced by politics in New York City in the 1880s, for example, would have helped only one percent of the work force. Significant expansions of the municipal work force had to be financed by increasing taxation, a politically dangerous thing to do even then. Far from responding uncritically to the needs of their voters, the bosses had to think constantly about how to use their limited supplies of rewards. They had to know which political competitors they must placate and which they could afford to snub; which supporters to reward with jobs and which to give only a bucket of coal; which request to respond to and which to refuse. Both the pressure to win elections to maintain control of patronage resources and the need to generate funds to finance other kinds of political rewards led some politicians into illegal activities. Close elections were sometimes "won" by stuffing ballot boxes with fraudulent ballots, hiring voters (called "repeaters") to vote as many times as possible on the same day, or driving the supporters of opponents away from the polls by physical force. Politicians sometimes raised funds for partisan activities by demanding kickbacks from contractors or fees from corporations or by accepting bribes to keep the police from enforcing laws against prostitution, gambling, or other illegal activities. And political bosses sometimes enriched themselves by forcing franchise holders to give them shares of stock in their companies or by buying real estate whose value they knew would soon increase because it was needed for municipal projects.

When these kinds of activities were exposed, they aggravated a second problem for the machine builders, the fragile political legitimacy of the system of patronage democracy itself. Although millions voted through the parties, the electorate was by no means immune to the attacks on the partisan system that began in the 1880s and rose to a fevered pitch by the turn of the century. Critics of partisanship itself, advocates of workers, farmers, and women, partisans who didn't get what they thought they deserved in the way of patronage, ordinary citizens shocked by revelations of electoral fraud or political corruption all added their voices at various times to criticism of the system: The parties were too concerned with patronage or too closely aligned with business and therefore not devoted enough to solving the problems of the day. Meanwhile political reforms aimed at undermining partisanship and the political machines began to move through the federal and state governments. Civil service laws that took government employment out of the hands of the parties began to pass. State after state adopted the so-called Australian or secret ballot, which shifted the right to print and distribute ballots from the parties to state and local government. Closer government supervision of partisan primaries began to remove fraud and violence from these elections and to give opponents of machines the opportunity to challenge them within the parties themselves. Some advocates proposed woman suffrage as an antimachine reform on the grounds that women would not vote to sustain corruption. All of these ideological and structural attacks made it difficult for citywide machines to be built and, from time to time, also facilitated the ouster from power (temporarily at least) of even well-entrenched machines like Tammany.[10]

While they lasted, powerful political machines made the most of the possibilities for organization and political strategy within the system of patronage democracy. They were not necessarily the best or most efficient way to run cities, and they did not emerge simply in response to the needs of the urban electorate. What we see in the story of George Washington Plunkitt and Tammany Hall is, therefore, not the story of a natural outgrowth of urban conditions but the successful building of a political organization.

A LIFE IN THE MACHINE: PLUNKITT IN THE TAMMANY ORGANIZATION

There is no doubt where George Washington Plunkitt stood on the issues proposed by reformers. He opposed every one of these reforms and indeed had little love for reformers themselves either. For Plunkitt, civil service was "the biggest fraud of the age," stricter state supervision of primary elections was "dangerous," woman suffrage was "unamerican," and reformers didn't understand that politics was "a business." Plunkitt believed fully in the

Opened just in time for the Democratic National Convention of 1868, this building, on 14th Street between Irving Place and Third Avenue, was the home of the Tammany Society and the Tammany Democracy until 1928.

system of patronage democracy; in fact, he had made a career out of it in the most famous and best-organized political machine in the country, and he had no use for changes that might undermine it. He first ran for office in 1866 when he was twenty-four years old, and he held or was running for some kind of political position for the next forty years, up to and including 1905, the year *Plunkitt of Tammany Hall* was published.

Plunkitt was born in New York City in 1842 in an area of the upper West Side of Manhattan that was probably a collection of shacks built by Irish squatters. The area was later incorporated into Central Park at about West 84th Street. Although he never mentioned his family in public, the 1850 census found him living with his parents, Patrick and Sarah Plunket (he would later change the spelling of his last name), his twin brother, David, and a brother three years younger named Dan. His parents were both born in Ireland, neither could read, and his father worked as a laborer. In spite of their own lack of education and their probably difficult economic circumstances, the Plunkets had both George and David in school that year. George attended public schools for about five years, from age six to eleven, and then he began driving horse carts for construction projects in his neighborhood. He was later apprenticed to a brush maker and then to a butcher. By 1865 he owned his own butcher shop in the Washington Market, a sprawling collection of shops located along the Hudson River between Fulton and Vesey streets in lower Manhattan that was one of the main places New Yorkers purchased their meat, fish, and produce. Around 1876 he sold the shop and went into contracting and real estate investment on the middle and upper West Side of Manhattan. Some accounts say that he was involved in the building of docks and piers along the Hudson River there. He later became a director of the Riverside Bank and claimed to have become a millionaire through these activities. At some point he was married and had one child, although he rarely spoke of this family either.[11]

Plunkitt's public political career began with an unsuccessful run for the New York State Assembly in 1866. He won the same position in 1868 and was reelected in 1869 and 1870. While still serving in the state legislature, he was elected in 1870 to the first of four one-year terms as a New York City alderman. He would later claim the distinction of having held four offices simultaneously in the early 1870s—assemblyman, county supervisor, alderman, and police magistrate—and he was also a deputy commissioner of street cleaning for six years in that decade. First elected to the New York State Senate in 1883, he served until he was defeated for renomination in 1887. He was elected again to the Senate in 1891 but stepped down for reasons of health in 1893. Reelected to the Senate in 1899, he served there until he was defeated in 1904. Plunkitt never explained why he first went into politics, but he never forgot why he lost his first race and won his second. In his first unsuccessful race in 1866 he ran without the endorsement of Tammany Hall; in the second he ran with it. For the rest of his life Plunkitt would be a Tammany Hall candidate.

For readers of *Plunkitt of Tammany Hall* today, "Tammany Hall" itself may be the most confusing thing about the book. In Plunkitt's day Tammany Hall meant two different things. One was a building called Tammany Hall that was owned by the Tammany Society or Columbian Order, a men's benevolent organization like today's Masons or Knights of Columbus. The other Tammany Hall was a faction of the New York City Democratic party that rented its headquarters and meeting space in the Tammany Hall building from the Tammany Society. This was the Tammany Hall political machine. Plunkitt belonged to both the benevolent society and the political party and rose to positions of responsibility in each. For our purposes, we will call the political party faction the Tammany Democracy and the benevolent organization the Tammany Society.[12]

In Plunkitt's day the Democratic party of New York City was divided into a number of competing factions based on such things as social class, ethnicity, geography, and political positions on issues. These factions—frequently named after the halls where they met—battled for control of party nominations for political office and the distribution of patronage following a political victory. The Tammany Hall faction was dominated by the Irish, and most of its leadership worked full time in politics. By the turn of the century Tammany Hall had become the most powerful faction, and until the 1930s it was almost synonymous with the Democratic party in the city.[13]

Plunkitt entered the Tammany Democracy when it was being run by the infamous "Boss" William Marcy Tweed. Tweed set the stereotype for the powerful, extravagant, and corrupt boss that the Tammany Democracy spent the rest of the century trying to live down. Tweed had entered politics after achieving popularity in the city's volunteer fire companies. In succession he was elected city alderman and United States congressman. In 1857 he was elected to a newly created bipartisan board of supervisors for the county of New York (then including only the city), which had been set up by the state to control the city's administration. It was this board that in 1858 authorized spending $250,000 for a new courthouse (later called the Tweed courthouse) that was finally finished in 1872 at a cost of $12.5 million. Tweed used kickbacks from this project and funds from wealthy supporters both to enrich himself and to support his bid for political power. By the late 1860s he was simultaneously county supervisor, superintendent of public works, state senator, chairman of the Tammany Democracy, and head of the Tammany Society. With these positions he was able to arrange to have his supporters elected or appointed mayor and city controller as well as to propose bills in the state legislature to help further consolidate his power. He lived flamboyantly, flaunting his newfound wealth and hobnobbing with the elite of New York City. In 1871 his enemies released records of his financial depredations to the *New York Times*. As a result of this exposure Tweed was arrested; after a series of legal maneuvers and a dramatic escape, he died in prison in 1878.[14]

We do not know exactly what Plunkitt thought of Tweed. It is clear that in the early 1870s, Plunkitt too was following the pattern of multiple of-ficeholding that Tweed pioneered. But by 1870 Plunkitt was a member of an anti-Tweed faction in Tammany called the Young Democracy, and in a climactic series of votes in the state legislature by which Tweed further consolidated his power, Plunkitt voted against the boss. To Tweed's enemies within Tammany, the boss failed in two ways. First, he placed himself above the organization both in his one-man rule and in his undisciplined personal behavior which drew negative attention to Tammany. Second, he failed to build an organization with strong political roots. Tweed's organization is known as a "ring" (not a machine) because it really involved only coopera-tion and cover-up among Tweed and a handful of his supporters who held critical municipal offices.[15]

After the downfall of Tweed the next three bosses of the Tammany Democracy—"Honest" John Kelly (1874–1886), Richard Croker (1886–1901), and Charles Francis Murphy (1903–1924)—worked to transform it into a disciplined and hierarchical organization in which, as an admirer put it, the leader could "cast 110,000 votes as easily as his own." These votes would allow the Tammany Democracy to triumph over its enemies within the Democratic party by nominating the candidates it chose for the party's state and local primaries and then to elect those candidates over their Republican or other opponents in the general elections. Those officials would then be expected to appoint Tammany supporters to positions at their disposal and to make policy favorable to Tammany's interests.[16]

The Tammany organization in the era after Tweed can best be thought of as a pyramid. At the apex was the boss. At the next level down was the executive committee, made up of the thirty or so elected leaders of the Tammany Democracy in the city's state Assembly districts. In cooperation with the boss, the executive committee made decisions for the whole organi-zation at the same time as its members organized Tammany activities in their own districts and maintained district Tammany clubhouses. From 1880 until 1905 Plunkitt was a member of this committee because he was the leader of one of the three Assembly districts that made up his state senatorial district. The organization's next level down was the General Committee, six to seven thousand members strong. This group included the election district captains and their assistants, who worked on Tammany's behalf at the block and neighborhood level, and it was also open to anyone else willing to pay the five-dollar annual membership fee in hopes of receiving preference for patronage jobs. Plunkitt appointed more than seventy election district captains in his district and they in turn appointed their own assistants. The district captains informed the district leader of the political situation in their neighborhoods and helped to get out the primary and general election vote. Not surprisingly, these men expected to receive patronage jobs or other opportunities in return for their services.[17]

At the very bottom of this pyramid were the voters, with whom Tammany had a complicated relationship. The machine needed votes to retain political power, of course, but it existed to shape and channel those votes. Luckily for the machine, thousands of men already voted for the Democratic party and worked on behalf of the Tammany Democracy out of a loyalty based on the party's ideology, stance on issues, or leadership. Some saw the Democratic party as the party of the common person and associated the Republicans with big business, an impression confirmed by the support of the Republicans for a high protective tariff. Some opposed the Republican-sponsored policies for reconstructing the South after the Civil War and voted Democratic because they saw the Republicans as too protective of black people. Many naturalized immigrant voters supported Tammany because its leadership was composed of Irish and German immigrants like themselves. All Tammany had to do was get these voters to the polls. For those who needed further inducement, both Croker and Plunkitt held out the possibility of a share in the spoils that went to the victorious party, although it is not clear how much of this patronage remained after it had trickled down to the electorate through the other levels of the organization. In an article published in 1892, for example, Croker declared that Tammany "stands by its friends" and that if the result was that "all the employees of the city government from the Mayor to the porter who makes the fire in his office" should be members of the Tammany organization, "this would not be to their discredit." Both Croker and Plunkitt genuinely believed that voters wanted something concrete and material (or at least the prospect of the same) out of politics. It was no coincidence, however, that men whose jobs depended on political victory would work very hard for the political organization that appointed them.[18]

LIFE IN THE DISTRICT

The Assembly district that Plunkitt led for Tammany was one in which the promise of a job could mean a great deal because it was located in an area of Manhattan called "a hotbed of unemployment" by investigators writing after the turn of the twentieth century. Although the boundaries of his district shifted from time to time because of legislative reapportionment, from the 1860s until his death in 1924 Plunkitt lived within the area bounded by West 51st Street on the north, West 49th Street on the south, Eighth Avenue on the east, and the Hudson River on the west. This was at the northern end of the middle West Side, a mixed residential and industrial area that extended roughly from 34th to 54th Street between Eighth Avenue and the Hudson River. Known more popularly as "Hell's Kitchen," this area was famous for its concentration of Irish immigrants, brawling street gangs, and colorful personalities from all walks of life, including crime and sports. Beneath this colorful image, however, its overwhelmingly immigrant population struggled to carve out a life of working-class respectability in the midst of underemployment and inadequate tenement housing.[19]

Industries moved into the middle West Side in the years after the Civil War because of its cheap land and its proximity to the river, and as the century went on the area became home to carpet and twine factories, slaughterhouses, iron and steel foundries, breweries, piano works, gas works, and railroad yards. By 1910 the three hundred industrial establishments in this area employed about eleven thousand workers (roughly 80 percent of them men), the largest employers being in piano manufacturing, printing, and metalwork. But the most highly skilled workers in these plants did not live in the area, and the largest number of middle West Side residents worked in lower-paying and more casual jobs. For men living in the area, the most numerous occupations were teamster, building trades worker, laborer, and longshoreman; most women did "day work" (cleaning, ironing, and so on in private homes), public cleaning, and laundry or hotel work.[20]

By all indications, much of the district was hardworking but underemployed. Detailed employment histories of area residents revealed working careers among both men and women that were interrupted by the irregularities of employment, illness, and injury. Few men were able to support their families unassisted and so a large percentage of married women with children worked. Thirty percent of the children at the 53rd Street public school and almost 40 percent at the 38th Street school lived with mothers who worked outside the home at a time when the national rate of employment among married women with children was about 4 percent. Even in families where both parents worked, however, average incomes hovered around a minimal subsistence level. In part for this reason, most of the district's population lived in three-to-five-story tenements housing from six to twenty families each.[21]

In spite of its poverty, the middle West Side was no cultural wasteland. There was, to begin with, remarkable cultural homogeneity in the area because it was composed overwhelmingly of Catholic immigrants and their children. In 1900 the largest ethnic groups in the area—together accounting for more than 60 percent of its residents—were the Irish and the Germans, who had begun arriving in the mid-nineteenth century. Because the latter were from the Catholic regions of southern Germany, intermarriage between the two groups was high. These immigrant groups now looked disparagingly on the more recently arrived Italians and Poles, calling them "foreigners." One reason for this attitude was a surprisingly high rate of permanence in the area among its residents. At a time when upwards of 60 percent of some urban neighborhoods would turn over every ten years, as many as 50 to 60 percent of residents of the middle West Side surveyed in 1910 had lived in the area for twenty years or more, and a good many of these had actually been born in the district.[22]

Eighth Avenue was the middle-class "main street" of this area, the place where those with the means and need caught the streetcars for downtown Manhattan, shopped, or socialized. Observers called this street the "Broadway and Fifth Avenue" of the middle West Side. A walk westward traversed the social geography of the district. Between Eighth and Ninth avenues the area's middle class lived in spacious flats or multistory, single-family dwellings. The tenements began west of Ninth Avenue, and the industrial works crowded out residential areas between Eleventh Avenue and the river. The elevated railway (the El) ran above Ninth Avenue, and the New York Central Railroad went up the middle of Eleventh Avenue beginning at 30th Street, so the areas around these avenues took on an air of dirt, noise, and danger. The commercial heart of the working-class area was Ninth and Tenth avenues, where the residents of the tenements went about their shopping and socializing. On Saturday nights pushcart vendors set up a street market known as "Paddy's Market" under the El along Ninth Avenue.[23]

The similarities between Plunkitt's life and those of his constituents were important political assets for him. Because he was the son of Irish immigrants, a longtime resident of the area, and a practicing Roman Catholic, he shared the ethnicity and permanence of many and the religion of most of his neighbors. These attributes alone were sufficient to secure the votes of many. The permanence that he shared with many district residents was a double advantage because it gave him many years to get to know the voters and also ensured that his favors for them would not be wasted. Permanent residents would repeatedly repay favors at the polls and continue to tell the stories of the boss's generosity (or their influence or "pull" with him) long after.[24]

At the same time, however, the differences between his life and theirs were potential political liabilities and as time went on the economic and social distance between Plunkitt and many of his constituents seemed to grow. The house to which he moved in the 1890s (and where he lived until his death) was a multistory, single-family townhouse (with room for the maid he hired) in the best part of the district, at 323 West 51st Street, between Eighth and Ninth avenues. His political headquarters, Washington Hall, was located not in the grimy working-class area of the district but at 781 Eighth Avenue on the area's "Broadway and Fifth Avenue." In all the accounts of Plunkitt's life after 1880—his own or others—there is not a single mention of him actually going to work as a contractor or, for that matter, as anything other than a ward boss.[25]

While Plunkitt's constituents trudged off to work on the docks on the Hudson if they were male or to scrub the steps of a Broadway theater if they were female, his day began with reading the newspapers at home. That done, it was off to the neighborhood barber for a shave. All his life Plunkitt was known to be something of a dandy, proud in particular of his whiskers, which went from a full beard to the long muttonchop sideburns known as dundrearies to just a mustache. He usually wore a pearl gray homburg and one account said he dressed more like a dancing master than a man with contracts for work on the docks. Whiskers tended to, Plunkitt usually took the streetcar downtown to conduct business. One stop was his "informal headquarters" at Graziano's bootblack stand in the old county courthouse, where he would hold forth on one of the shoe shine chairs. Another frequent stop was at Tammany Hall itself, which was on 14th Street between Irving Place and Third Avenue. These trips concluded, he returned to the district where he could be found at Washington Hall or nearby most afternoons and evenings.[26]

The reason Plunkitt sold his butcher shop around 1876 was that he had found he could make a living in and through politics. Not surprisingly, therefore, his career was marked by controversy. In 1872 he was indicted but never tried for selling street railway franchises as an alderman. In the 1880s and 1890s he was alleged to be on the payroll of the New York Central Railroad while he was serving in the state legislature. The newspapers charged that he had deals with the city Department of Streets, which rented properties from him at high rates, with the Dock Department, from which he received construction contracts, and with the city assessor, who underassessed his properties to reduce his taxes. In 1905 other politicians claimed that Plunkitt sold nominations for office over which he had control. In spite of these complaints, however, by the turn of the century Plunkitt was both a powerful politician and, he claimed, a millionaire.[27]

Plunkitt was undoubtedly a good organization man. He served loyally as a district leader under three different Tammany bosses and held a variety of positions in the Tammany hierarchy. He was often the chairman of the Tammany Democracy's election committee, which was responsible for interpreting election law to other party members, and he was always chairman of the Tammany transportation committee, which arranged the transportation of delegates to the state and national conventions of the Democratic party. Another sign of the respect in which he was held by his peers was his leadership roles in the Tammany Society, a kind of "old boys club" for prominent Democrats complete with secret rituals, regalia, passwords, and signs. The organization was founded in 1789 and named after a legendary Indian chief of the Delaware tribe, Tammanend. Its rituals combined patriotic and pseudo-Indian themes. Internally, for example, it was divided into thirteen tribes (the number of original states) ruled by sachems or chiefs. These sachems named a Grand Sachem who ran the organization with them. In the 1860s Boss Tweed consolidated his power by being elected both head of the Tammany Democracy and Grand Sachem of the Tammany Society, and from then on there was a close link between the leadership of the benevolent organization and that of the party faction. The Tammany Society was a much more exclusive organization than the Tammany Democracy. From its founding until 1926, only about six thousand men were invited to join the society, a process that required nomination of the new member by one of the old members and a vote on the nomination at three successive meetings. Plunkitt was initiated into the society in 1882, and in 1897 he was elected to a one-year term as a sachem. He was elected a sachem again in 1900 and remained one until his death. In 1902 he was elected Father of the Council of Sachems, in which capacity he conducted the meetings of the council; he also held that position until his death.[28]

As Plunkitt traveled from Washington Hall to Tammany Hall, he moved among men remarkably like himself. Many of the other leaders of the Tammany Democracy had similar careers, and a good number of them also claimed to be millionaires and were proud of it. These men were linked by a history of social and political struggle in the past and cultural and political values in the present. There was, in fact, exceptional overlap in membership, organization, framework, and guiding philosophy among the three organizations that claimed and rewarded Plunkitt's allegiance. The Roman Catholic Church, Tammany Democracy, and Tammany Society were all dominated by Irish immigrants and their children in membership and leadership; their leadership was exclusively male; they were all organized hierarchically, with authority designed to flow from the top down; and the leadership of each was convinced that there was no "salvation," either religious or political, outside of its organization.[29]

The Irish-American leaders of the church, the bosses of the Tammany Democracy, and the sachems of the Tammany Society had all known poverty and marginality, but not for some time. As they looked around in the 1880s and 1890s they saw themselves as part of a growing middle-class community that had made its way by sticking together and building organizations that allowed them to carve a niche for themselves within the existing economic and political structures. While these leaders stood shoulder to shoulder in defense of their immigrant membership, they also stood in firm opposition to popular political movements they did not control, such as the labor-backed New York mayoral campaign of Henry George in 1886, the populist movement in the 1890s, and the socialist movement after the turn of the century. These men were all Democrats, but not democrats; the idea of a kind of grassroots democracy was totally foreign to them because that way led to both religious apostasy and ticket-splitting, the greatest sins, respectively, to the church and the party.[30]

As Plunkitt moved up the ranks of Tammany, he walked a fine line in his district between being a local boy who made good and a politician who forgot his roots. The difference came down to three things: service, generosity, and the common touch in both reputation and reality. The social surveys of the area claimed that the "average opinion" of the neighborhood was represented in the Irish-American mothers, described as "rough and ready Irish women who give themselves no airs and 'don't pretend to be better than the people they was raised with.'" To the husbands of women like these (who actually did the voting) Plunkitt was entitled to his millions—however gotten—as long as he worked hard on their behalf, shared some of his wealth, and didn't put on airs. He clearly understood all this, claiming in one conversation with Riordon that "nobody ever saw me putting on any style" and noting in another that there was an implicit contract between boss and ward according to which the boss was owed support as long as he "hustles around and gets all the jobs possible for his constituents."[31]

Luckily for Plunkitt, relatively small amounts of money from him could have a significant impact on his reputation for generosity in his district in areas other than employment. Average rents in the tenement areas ranged from $115 to $165 per year, so $10 could cover a month's rent for those in the poorest housing. The fine for a juvenile offense might be $3. These were significant sums for the poorest families in the district, some of whom might bring in only $6 or $7 a week, although they were pocket change for a generous district leader who claimed to be a millionaire.[32]

While it was absolutely crucial for Plunkitt to claim that he was constantly working on behalf of his district, there is some evidence to the contrary in surveys of working women and juvenile delinquents in the middle West Side conducted in 1910. A study of 370 working mothers who were among the most needy and most permanent residents of the area revealed that not a single one of them or their husbands had ever received a job—or anything else—from a boss. A similar study of 183 families of juvenile delinquents found that only two had ever received help from a boss or precinct captain when their children got in trouble with the law. And in one of these cases the boss paid the fine of one boy and left the other in jail because his parents did not have enough pull with the boss. Not all of these people lived in Plunkitt's Assembly district, but the question of Plunkitt's generosity would continue to be an issue among both reformers and his enemies within Tammany.[33]

GEORGE W. PLUNKITT,
Sachem.

By the turn of the twentieth century this photograph of Plunkitt—portraying him as handsome, forthright, and upstanding—was the one that he supplied to publications requesting a portrait.

THE BATTLE OVER THE
MEANING OF THE BOSS

Plunkitt's skills were warmly admired in the Tammany machine and just as warmly denounced by political reformers. In one of its frequent portrayals of the leaders of the Tammany Democracy, *The Tammany Times,* the machine's official newspaper, declared in 1895 that Plunkitt was "one of nature's noblemen" who had "devoted the best portion of his life to the interests of his constituents." According to this account, "the name of George W. Plunkitt stands as a guarantee of good faith." Writing at almost the same time, political reformer and New York *Evening Post* editor E. L. Godkin declared that Plunkitt was "the greatest hustler in Tammany Hall," with a reputation as a state senator in Albany that was "most unsavory."[34]

While the machine system might work for Plunkitt and at least some of his constituents, there was strong agreement among the generation of reformers and journalists such as British author James Bryce, Godkin, or New York reform mayor Seth Low that it was no way to run a city. Bryce's classic analysis of American political institutions, *The American Commonwealth* (1888), declared that American city government was the "one conspicuous failure of the United States" because of its domination by corrupt political machines like the Tammany Democracy. Godkin argued that Tammany had long since ceased to be a political organization—"that is, an association for the spread of any set of particular opinions or for producing cooperation in anything that could be called political agitation"—and was now simply "an organization of clever adventurers, most of them in some degree criminal, for the control of the ignorant and viscous vote of the city in an attack on the property of the taxpayers." In part because of its makeup and intentions, Tammany stayed in power "not through its own strength, but through the supineness, indifference, and optimism of the rest of the community."[35]

Stimulated in part by Bryce's work and in part by his own sense of a growing complacency about Tammany in New York and the nation, Godkin decided to declare journalistic war on Tammany in the 1890s. Believing that the three things a Tammany leader hated most were "the penitentiary, honest industry, and biography," he opened his campaign with the "Tammany Biographies," a set of biographies of the Tammany leaders that first appeared in 1890 and was reprinted as a pamphlet throughout the decade. Summarizing the backgrounds of the current twenty-eight members of the Tammany executive committee, Godkin claimed that all were "professional politicians," that twenty-five of them were current or former officeholders, nine were current or former liquor dealers, nine current or former gamblers or owners of gambling houses, seven former "pugilists" or "toughs," and so on. Not on the list, Godkin noted, was "a single man who owes his eminence to anything save his skill in Tammany politics." According to Godkin's account, Plunkitt was in politics "as a business," had "no hesitation in using his position for his private gain," and was a "thoroughly bad Senator."[36]

For a man like Godkin, the machines were the temporary result of political institutional conditions and of the lies and intimidation of unscrupulous politicians who were subverting the American political process. He was, therefore, a strong supporter of reforms such as state supervision of primary elections, civil service, and the election to office of men of the "better sort" (that is, upper middle class like himself). His journalistic exposure of the men and methods of Tammany was designed specifically to arouse the better sort to take action toward removing Tammany from power, and it did have an effect. Godkin's campaigns, combined with a state investigation that revealed massive political corruption within the police force, stimulated the growth of reform organizations in the 1890s and resulted in the election of mayors William L. Strong in 1894 and Seth Low in 1901, both of whom vowed to drive Tammany and its ways out of city government. But neither of these reform mayors was reelected.[37]

Realizing the potential power of these attacks, Tammany boss Richard Croker responded by starting an official weekly newspaper for the machine in 1892 called *The Tammany Times* and by authorizing a new history of Tammany Hall that was first serialized in *The Tammany Times* and then published as a book in 1901. Week after week the *Times* stressed the machine's link with the more distinguished national leaders of the Democratic party and described the leaders of Tammany in a way diametrically opposed to that of Godkin. Photos of prominent Democrats like Grover Cleveland, William Jennings Bryan, and Woodrow Wilson frequently appeared on the front page of the *Times,* and inside the leaders of Tammany were described in glowing terms as "manly" men of broad vision and democratic commitment. According to the *Times* Croker, for example, owed his popularity to "his manly spirit, fixed resolve, indomitable will and his unswerving honesty of purpose in his protective and aggressive warfare for the people's rights." And Plunkitt was described as "an excellent debater, an argumentative and forcible speaker, carrying with him that earnestness which is almost certain of conviction . . . and a personal bearing to all with whom he comes in contact calculated to rally strong support." The theme of the new history of Tammany was that there had been a blot of corruption during the days of the notorious Tweed but that Tammany had purified itself and thus was now the best vehicle for reform in New York City.[38]

Croker reiterated these themes in many interviews he granted to journalists. The most influential interview was conducted by William T. Stead and published in the London *Review of Reviews* in October 1897. Stead began by asking Croker whether there was anything in his political career that he regretted having done. Croker's solemn answer was "No sir. Not one. For I have done only good all my life." The proof of his good deeds, according to Croker, was the persistence of Tammany Hall itself. Because "those things that are rotten do not last," he claimed, Tammany could not have had the power it had for as long as it had if it had been built on dishonesty or corruption. It survived because its brand of politics was more in conformity with human nature and because of the various services it provided to New York society. According to Croker, a "strong effective party machine" was "essential to the safe working of popular institutions," and the much derided "spoils system" was the only way to motivate and guarantee people's participation in political affairs. Furthermore, for the sake of winning elections Tammany performed an important service by Americanizing immigrants. While there was not a reformer in New York City who would "shake hands with" the thousands of foreigners arriving in the city, Croker asserted, Tammany looked after the immigrants "for the sake of their vote, graft[ed] them upon the Republic, [made] citizens of them in short."[39]

Croker's themes of his own frankness and the machine's kindness quickly made their way into the journalistic coverage of the Tammany Democracy beginning with Hartley Davis's frankly admiring portrait, "Tammany Hall, the Most Perfect Political Organization in the World," in *Munsey's* magazine in October 1900 and continuing in 1901 in William Allen White's "Croker" in the February *McClure's* magazine and in Alfred Henry Lewis's biography *Richard Croker* published in May. Each of these works cited the Stead interview with Croker, praised Croker for his frank avowal of Tammany's desire for the spoils of office, and rooted the power and persistence of the machine in the services it provided to the voters. Davis claimed that while Tammany politicians were motivated by "no patriotic concern" and were in politics "for what there was in it," they nonetheless did "wonderful work" for their constituents. In "relieving distress, in providing for daily wants, in furthering ambitions, in helping men out of their troubles and in assisting them to get on in the world," he wrote, Tammany did "more for the daily personal comfort, happiness, and well being of the average tenement dweller than all the charitable and philanthropic institutions in New York." In part on this basis White flatly contradicted Godkin, arguing that Tammany persisted "by its virtues and in spite of its vices." Lewis and White also added an important secondary theme to the discussion by crediting Tammany's kindness and political socialization with preventing radicalism from taking root among the immigrants. "Take away the steel hoops of Tammany from the social dynamite, and let it go kicking around under the feet of any cheap agitator who may come by with his head in the clouds, and then look out for fireworks," White wrote, while Lewis similarly extolled the machine's "suppressive influence."[40]

In these political and journalistic battles between bosses and reformers it was not always clear who, if anyone, spoke for the interests of the urban population itself. Calls for electoral reform, civil service, an end to corruption, or government by the better sort surely did little to alleviate the immediate needs of those in the city who faced unemployment, poor housing, and poverty. But political machines like Tammany clearly wanted to shape, rather than be shaped by, the needs of the voters, some bosses undoubtedly worked harder for themselves than for their constituents, and there was no evidence other than the testimony of the bosses themselves for Tammany's frankness and kindness.

This concern for who was standing with and responding to the needs of the urban population motivated two of the most famous evaluations of the machine and reform ever written: "Why the Ward Boss Rules," by the social worker and reformer Jane Addams, and "New York: Good Government in Danger," by the muckraking journalist Lincoln Steffens. The influence of these articles stemmed from the backgrounds and the analyses of the authors. Both Addams and Steffens were well-known opponents of political corruption and both wrote about machines as part of their broader effort to describe a new kind of urban reform politics, one concerned less with the structure or personnel of government and more with its scope. They did not share the faith of men like Godkin and Bryce in civil service, ballot or primary reform, or government by the "better sort." For them a "reformed" government was one that met the human needs of its constituents.[41]

Jane Addams had come to Chicago in 1889 and opened Hull House, a social settlement house that offered help to the immigrants and the poor in Chicago's nineteenth ward. She became famous in Chicago for, among other things, her strenuous criticism of the corruption and malfeasance of Johnny Powers, the alderman from and political boss of the ward in which Hull House was located. With the help of the Chicago Municipal Voters' League, Addams organized unsuccessful political campaigns against Powers in 1896 and 1898. Because she lived among those whom bosses and reformers claimed to help and because she had worked so hard against a ward boss, her views were given wide legitimacy. "Why the Ward Boss Rules" caused a sensation because its startling argument was the same as Croker's—that ward bosses ruled not through faulty institutions, the ignorance of foreigners, or the indifference of the "better sort" (as Bryce or Godkin might have argued) but because they practiced "simple kindness" in the wards day in and day out. According to Addams, the desperate situation of the urban poor gave them many opportunities to practice "simple kindness" to one another and thereby to develop an ethical standard for which apparent kindness was the test. To these "simple" people, the corrupt boss, unlike the hectoring reformer, practiced the kindness that the immigrant poor admired. The kindly alderman stayed in office because he bailed out his constituents, found them jobs, paid the rent for those too poor to do so themselves, attended weddings, christenings, and funerals, got railroad passes for those needing to travel, bought "tickets galore" for benefit entertainments, and provided prizes and spent dramatically at the neighborhood bazaars.[42]

Addams's article said nothing about her long campaign against her own local boss, and she discussed political corruption only briefly. She emphasized the kindness of the boss in part because her article was also designed to send a message to other reformers. "If we discover that men of low ideals and corrupt practice are forming popular political standards simply because such men stand by and for and with the people," she wrote, "then nothing remains but to obtain a like sense of identification before we can hope to modify ethical standards."

The question of municipal political ethics was also much on the mind of Lincoln Steffens as he traveled around the country surveying the state of local politics in 1902. Steffens had come to New York in 1892 and begun working as a reporter for the New York *Evening Post* that year, covering reform campaigns against Tammany, among other things. He left the *Post* in 1897 to become city editor of the New York *Commercial Advertiser,* and he joined *McClure's* magazine in 1901. In October 1902 Steffens published in *McClure's* the first of what would be seven articles on the state of corruption in municipal politics in America. His report on New York City was the last of the series, published in November 1903. These articles were collected and published together as the book *The Shame of the Cities* in 1904.[43]

The New York article was actually an attempt to assess the prospects for the continuation of the reform surge that had elected Seth Low to the mayoralty in 1901, and Steffens argued, like Addams, that reformers had something to learn from the techniques of machine politicians. According to Steffens the problem with the New York reform movement was that it was businesslike but not democratic; Mayor Seth Low applied excellent principles to the management of municipal government but was unable to build a democratic political movement to support reform. Steffens saw a better understanding of "practical" democratic politics in the Tammany Democracy. Tammany bosses made no bones about their corruption but ruled through the suffrage of the people because they spread the fruits of their corruption widely. In a manner strikingly similar to that of Addams, Davis, and the others, Steffens provided a long list of the kindnesses of the ward bosses and argued that "Tammany kindness was real kindness and went far" and its power, "gathered up cheaply like garbage in the districts," was passed on through the organization to the boss. It was "living government, extra-legal, but very actual," and Tammany was, therefore, the most democratic of all the corrupt urban political organizations Steffens had studied.[44]

However, Steffens's article also contained a scathing attack on the way Tammany financed its kindness through corrupt deals that brought in "untold millions of dollars a year." Steffens's catalog of this corruption was long and detailed, and it mentioned bribes to the bosses and the police from saloons and houses of gambling and prostitution, kickbacks on public works, profiting on inside information about public improvements, and forcing corporations to allow Tammany leaders to buy stock. Considering all these sources of wealth Steffens thought it was no wonder that the members of the Tammany executive committee were wealthy, but as they grew wealthy ward bosses were likely to become cruel. "Their charity is real, at first. But they sell out their own people," Steffens wrote. "They do give them coal and help them in their private troubles, but, as they grow rich and powerful, the kindness goes out of the charity and they not only collect at their saloons or in rents—cash for their 'goodness'; they not only ruin fathers and sons and cause the troubles they relieve; they sacrifice the children in the schools; let the Health Department neglect the tenements, and, worst of all, plant vice in the neighborhood and in the homes of the poor." This, Steffens argued, was bad politics and in the end it would lead to Tammany's downfall if reformers could build a political movement that was both honest and committed to practical democratic politics.

Both Addams and Steffens wrote to offer hope to reformers. The seemingly omnipotent political machines had an Achilles' heel in their corruption, and reformers could take advantage of this weakness if they would propose that government itself develop social welfare–type programs to meet the real human needs of urban citizens. To make this point they emphasized—perhaps overemphasized—the "kindnesses" of the bosses and thus lent their stamp of approval to the ongoing revision of the image of the boss. By 1903 the journalistic portrayal of the machine had shifted from Godkin's band of "clever adventurers" to a group of frank, practical, kind (but unfortunately corrupt) do-gooders. The time was ripe for the transformation of George Washington Plunkitt into *Plunkitt of Tammany Hall.*

William L. Riordon, New York *Evening Post* reporter and editor of *Plunkitt of Tammany Hall,* was thirty-eight years old when this portrait was published in 1899. It is not known when the photo was taken.

BECOMING *PLUNKITT OF TAMMANY HALL*

The crucial middleman between these evaluations of ward bosses and the life of George Washington Plunkitt was William L. Riordon, whose life personally touched those on all sides of the debate over Tammany. When Riordon began his conversations with Plunkitt in 1897, he was a well-known political reporter covering the Tammany machine for the *Evening Post;* the editor of the *Post* was E. L. Godkin; and Riordon's office mate was Lincoln

Steffens. While Godkin's anti-Tammany fulminations were filling the editorial page, Riordon and Steffens worked together as reporters from 1892 to 1897, when there were only six full-time reporters on the paper's staff. It is quite likely that Steffens learned some things about the inner workings of Tammany from Riordon, and Riordon would later return the favor by focusing portions of *Plunkitt of Tammany Hall* on Steffens's book *The Shame of the Cities*.

Born in Richmond, Virginia, in 1861, Riordon, like Plunkitt, was an Irish-American and a Roman Catholic. Indeed, Riordon began studies at a seminary to become a Catholic priest but left to write for newspapers in Washington, D.C. He came to New York in 1886 and was a political reporter for the *Commercial Advertiser* for five years before joining the *Evening Post,* where he worked until his death in 1909. Riordon spent his years at the *Post* covering local politics except during 1899, when he covered the state legislature in Albany. He was also the New York correspondent for the *Boston Transcript.*[45]

Riordon was not just one of the hundreds of journalists in New York in his time, but one of the best known. He enjoyed high contemporary journalistic status by virtue of his selection by the *Post* to cover local politics. This beat was reserved for star reporters at the turn of the century. But in his 1922 history of the *Post,* Allen Nevins wrote that Riordon also was thought to be one of the "three most remarkable" reporters on the *Post* in the 1890s (Lincoln Steffens was one of the others). According to Nevins, who was a member of the editorial board of the *Post* when he wrote, Riordon "never failed to bring home news; if there was nothing in the assignment he went to cover, he would get a story as good or better somewhere else." Therefore, Riordon could always be counted on "to have something worthwhile up his sleeve" when the *Post* needed to fill the paper.[46]

Riordon undoubtedly got some of these stories at Tammany Hall, where he was both liked and respected. When he died, the *New York Times* noted that he was "closely identified with Tammany Hall affairs," and the *Post* reported that he was well liked by political leaders both in Tammany and on the Republican side and that "few other reporters held the leaders' confidence so unfailingly." Nevins thought that Riordon had been a member of Tammany Hall (although there is no evidence of this) and said he was "invaluable in getting material for assaults" on the machine but protected from resentment there by his fairness. After a critical story about Tammany by Riordon had appeared in the *Post,* no less a person than Tammany boss Richard Croker himself was supposed to have said, "He has to earn a living like the rest of us."[47]

There is no evidence that Riordon set out originally to write a book about Plunkitt. Their relationship probably began as one of mutual short-term advantage. A ward boss was never hurt by publicity about his power, practicality, or generosity, and Riordon's personal background and knowledge of (if not sympathy with) Tammany must have made him seem like an ideal vehicle for Plunkitt's political self-promotion. At the same time, a reporter could make money out of a relationship with a colorful, quotable figure. Reporters of Riordon's day were paid for the number of column inches of their writing that appeared in the paper. Given the ongoing controversy over the Tammany machine, Riordon's editors were likely to select for publication entertaining stories purporting to reveal the secrets of a ward boss.

Riordon, of course, controlled the timing and influenced the focus of the stories about Plunkitt by selecting those that would appear in the *Post* from his many conversations with Plunkitt. As far as we can tell, Riordon's first interview with Plunkitt was published in the *Post* around the time of municipal elections in 1897, and fifteen had been published by 1905. Most of these appeared in election years and contained Plunkitt's electoral predictions or postmortems in addition to snatches of his philosophy. The themes of the latter in these interviews were the necessity of the spoils system in general and Tammany in particular and the various ways civil service was "humbug," or fraud.[48]

When Riordon decided to produce a book out of Plunkitt's wisdom, he did not simply collect these interviews. None of the themes and phrases that made the book famous appeared in the interviews in the *Post;* there was, for example, no mention of honest and dishonest graft, Plunkitt's millions, reformers as "morning glories," the trouble with Lincoln Steffens, or Plunkitt's diary. Instead, Riordon added sections to the book that had never appeared before. The new sections included the first ("Honest Graft and Dishonest Graft"), the seventh ("On 'The Shame of the Cities' "), and the last ("Strenuous Life of the Tammany District Leader"). He then edited the previously published interviews to reflect the themes in these new sections.

Did Riordon invent these sections? The pressure to get one's work published led to the journalistic practice known among Riordon's contemporaries as "faking"—the manufacture of quotations to liven up a story. A 1905 article in *The Journalist,* a newspaper for reporters published in New York, deplored the fact that "you've got to fake to be entertaining enough to hold a job" and claimed that "nearly all of the newspaper stories of humorous every-day happenings are wholly imaginary, or built on slender foundations." And when Riordon died in 1909, *Editor and Publisher* attributed the famous phrases of the book to him, claiming, for example, that "he gave to the English speaking world the phrase 'honest graft' " and noting that Plunkitt was "made to say" what Riordon wrote. Because almost all of our knowledge of Plunkitt comes through Riordon, we may never be able to determine whether Riordon was a "fakir" (as it was spelled in those days). But we must understand that Riordon's portrait of Plunkitt was consciously composed out of the cultural materials at Riordon's disposal. These included Riordon's own experience of Plunkitt and Tammany Hall, of course, but also his reading of the works by other journalists and reformers on the political machine and the available literary stereotypes of the ward boss.[49]

Because so much of both fiction and nonfiction had been written about ward bosses and Tammany Hall by the time Riordon wrote, there was already a widely understood way to portray the typical—perhaps stereotypical—ward boss. A literary critic writing in 1904 noted that "the Tammany boss has always been, we have been led to believe, an essentially blunt, matter-of-fact, semi-humorous personage. He never really quite takes himself seriously. Like Byron's buccaneer, he's the mildest mannered man that ever scuttled a ship or cut a throat." In choosing this way to portray Plunkitt, Riordon rejected two other possibilities with which he was familiar: the portrayals of Plunkitt by both Godkin and *The Tammany Times*. For both literary and marketing purposes the portrait of Plunkitt in *The Tammany Times*—"an excellent debater, an argumentative and forcible speaker"—was too boring, while that of Godkin in the *Post*—"a thoroughly bad Senator"—was too harsh and off-putting.[50]

Riordon further rounded off Plunkitt's rough edges and tried to increase the readership for *Plunkitt of Tammany Hall* by focusing some of the new sections on Steffens and adding the excerpt from Plunkitt's diary. In 1903 *McClure's* magazine had more than three hundred seventy thousand subscribers and Steffens's series of articles on municipal corruption had been a sensation when originally published. The articles received even more attention when they were released together in the fall of 1904 as *The Shame of the Cities*. By making some portions of *Plunkitt of Tammany Hall* seem like Plunkitt's response to Steffens's charges of graft in Tammany Hall, Riordon both tried to attach his book to Steffens's star and constructed something that had not existed before: an "honest" grafter. At the turn of the century "graft" was a term that was widely used but not sharply defined, but "honest graft" was surely an oxymoron. The author of the 1901 book *The World of Graft* defined it as "a generic slang term for all kinds of theft and illegal practices generally." By having Plunkitt declare himself an honest grafter, Riordon portrayed him as frank (willing to admit he was a grafter) and self-conscious (knowing the difference between honest and dishonest graft, even if this was a meaningless distinction). By adding a diary of Plunkitt's kindnesses in the ward, Riordon further stressed his Robin Hood–like character. So far as we know there is no Plunkitt diary; Riordon simply reorganized the lists of kindnesses in the articles by Addams, Steffens, Davis, and the others into a diary form.[51]

THE ROLE OF *PLUNKITT OF TAMMANY HALL* IN PLUNKITT'S POLITICAL DOWNFALL

Riordon's portrait of Plunkitt was influenced not only by the things he added to the text but also by one significant thing that he kept out of it. For all of the talk about Plunkitt's political expertise, he had already suffered a serious defeat before the book went to press, and at the moment the book appeared he was engaged in a losing fight for his political life, a fight that was not helped by the appearance of the book itself.

Plunkitt's slide into local political oblivion began in November 1904 when he was defeated for reelection to his seat in the state Senate by a man half his age, a political newcomer, a college and law school graduate, and, perhaps worst of all, a Republican. Martin Saxe was born in 1874 and was raised in a neighborhood not far from Plunkitt's. He attended public schools in the district but then went to prep school and Princeton University, where he studied law, philosophy, history, and literature. He graduated from the New York Law School in 1897 and practiced law privately before joining the city corporation counsel's office in 1902 during the reform mayoralty of Seth Low. His job with the city was to collect personal property taxes that were in arrears, and his supporters claimed that he had collected $600,000 in back taxes during his two-year term, in contrast to his Tammany predecessor's collection of only $157,000 in four years.[52]

Saxe campaigned hard in the district, going door to door to meet voters and holding many meetings and rallies. His campaign was focused on two slogans: "Lift the Plunkitt Mortgage" and "Give Young Men a Chance." According to Saxe, Plunkitt's self-enriching deals in the state legislature had "mortgaged" the district to railroad and other interests at the same time as Plunkitt's twenty years of district leadership and six previous terms in the state Senate had prevented younger men from taking leadership there. "Plunkitt is so chock full of Plunkitt that he can't see anybody else," Saxe

---

Left: This photograph was the frontispiece of the 1905 edition of *Plunkitt of Tammany Hall*. It was posed to heighten Plunkitt's image as a Tammany boss by seating him on Graziano's bootblack stand, surrounding him with political cronies, and placing a top hat on his head. As a sachem of the Tammany Society, Plunkitt was required to wear a top hat in public once a year for the society's July 4 ceremonies, but that was the only time he did so. His own favorite photograph of himself at this time—on the cover and page 19 of this volume—can be seen in this photo hanging between the crossed flags.

claimed. "When a man rides roughshod over a district like this for years it's time he was stopped."[53]

Not surprisingly, Plunkitt had a hard time taking Saxe's campaign seriously. He said that he had met Saxe and thought he was a nice young man but that he had warned him not to invest too much money in the campaign because it was so hopeless. Portraying himself as the "father" of both his district and the entire West Side of the city, Plunkitt claimed that "the very cobble stones would rise up to defend and vote for" him. In fact, Plunkitt's vote totals in the three previous elections suggest that there was a strong opposition to him and that, like many machine politicians, he was a somewhat conservative mobilizer of votes. On average about eleven thousand voters from his senatorial district voted against him in each of the elections of 1898, 1900, and 1902—a loyal opposition. Furthermore, Plunkitt's own base of support was almost static. The votes for him in those elections were 14,883, 14,541, and 14,723, numbers that suggest that he had identified his supporters and gotten them to the polls but that his support was not growing. In spite of these signs, however, no one could have been more surprised than Plunkitt when Saxe won the 1904 election by more than six hundred votes.[54]

Some of Plunkitt's statements during the campaign raise questions about how good a "father" he had actually been to his district. He often seemed to claim that he deserved to continue representing the district because of the wealth he had accumulated. The *New York Times* reported that Plunkitt's "favorite way of expressing his confidence in his everlasting hold on his constituency was the statement that 'I am worth $3 million, and I would just like to see the man who would be able to beat me in my district.' " And the *Tribune* reported that, contrary to his claim of being generous, he was "notoriously 'thrifty,' and the voters of the district, having this in mind, are settling old scores." Was his self-proclaimed reputation for generosity and service exaggerated? This question would be the issue in Plunkitt's contest the next year, a bitter, unsuccessful fight to retain his Tammany leadership of the fifteenth Assembly district, a position he had held for more than twenty years.[55]

The day after Plunkitt's defeat by Saxe for the Senate, a wag placed a sign in Plunkitt's chair at the courthouse bootblack stand saying, "For Sale—Apply to Senator Martin Saxe." While this surely added insult to injury, more ominous was the statement by a supporter of Assemblyman Thomas J. "The" McManus on the day after the election that "Plunkitt will be knocked out of the leadership of the Fifteenth as well as out of the Senate." The 1904 election returns seemed to predict as much, because McManus's vote for Assembly in the fifteenth district was one thousand more than the total cast for Plunkitt for Senate in the same district. (Plunkitt's larger state

Senate district included three state Assembly districts.)[56] Furthermore, in 1898 the state legislature had passed a primary law requiring that elections within political organizations be supervised by the state. The 1905 election for Tammany Hall district leader would be the first with strong opposition to Plunkitt that would have its outcome monitored by the state.

McManus had been a thorn in Plunkitt's political side since McManus first won election to the state Assembly as an independent, non-Tammany candidate in 1891. Born in 1864, and thus twenty-two years younger than Plunkitt, McManus was an attorney with a reputation as an orator. After his 1891 election he carried on a series of unsuccessful campaigns for Assembly against candidates backed by Plunkitt. His closest later campaign came in 1899 when, running as a Republican, he came within seventy-one votes of defeating Plunkitt's handpicked Tammany candidate. Apparently bowing to the inevitable, Plunkitt backed McManus's successful Assembly campaigns after the turn of the century. Supported within the fifteenth district by his mother and six brothers—who were a formidable political force themselves—and his own political club, the Thomas J. McManus Association, McManus steadily built his political base against Plunkitt as he watched support for the older man wane. In June 1905 the McManus Association, not surprisingly, unanimously endorsed McManus in his bid for Plunkitt's Tammany Hall leadership of the district. At the McManus Association picnic that August, the ten thousand in attendance were led in the campaign song:

> Good-bye to Plunkitt boys,
> He used us like play toys;
> Now we'll stick to Tom McManus,
> For "The" is true blue.
> He'll stick to me and you
> So we'll chase old Plunkitt to Gowanus.[57]

The song jokingly conjured up Plunkitt's self-proclaimed worst nightmare and raised the point that would become the central issue of the campaign. Gowanus Bay was a body of water off Brooklyn, a place that Plunkitt had frequently said he hated because it was full of "hayseeds," or country bumpkins. (For Plunkitt everywhere outside of Manhattan was the "country.") To "chase old Plunkitt to Gowanus," then, meant to put him in exile in the worst place imaginable. Less humorous were the charges at the center of the campaign that Plunkitt had used his constituents, growing rich while doing little or nothing for them, and that Plunkitt made Tammany candidates for office pay him for their nominations. The first charge had also been a theme of Saxe's 1904 campaign, of course. This campaign was different, though, because those making the charges were Tammany insiders.

In a widely reported incident that may very well have been planned,

McManus confronted Plunkitt on the steps of police headquarters with the charge that he had forced McManus and the alderman from Plunkitt's district, Fred Richter, to pay $500 for their nominations for office. Plunkitt concluded the exchange with a remark that echoed one he made during the campaign against Saxe: "Ain't you ashamed of your dirty work trying to destroy an old man like me—a man who has given forty years to the Democratic Party and all his time to the people? I tell you I've got $2,000,000 and I'll spend them and go to the poorhouse or back to the Senate." The alderman, meanwhile, supported McManus's version, adding that all the people were "sore on" Plunkitt because "he makes no bones of saying that he's in politics for what he can get out of it for himself and his boy Georgie and his nephew."[58]

The complaints of McManus and Richter seemed confirmed when the book *Plunkitt of Tammany Hall* landed like a bombshell in the campaign. Tammany district leadership campaigns moved into their most intense stages in September. The 1905 election was scheduled for Tuesday, September 19. The book was released on September 1, and on September 2 and 3 the New York *World* ran excerpts from it and other newspapers followed suit. Although as late as September 6 Plunkitt said he had not read the book, he was clearly pleased by its appearance and delighted that it carried a "tribute" from Charles F. Murphy, who was then the leader of Tammany Hall. "I guess that's enough to hold 'The' McManus and them fellows for a while," Plunkitt reportedly said. There is no evidence that Riordon had timed the appearance of the book to damage Plunkitt. More likely the publication date was chosen by the publisher in an attempt to promote sales.[59]

What Plunkitt was not prepared for, however, was the effect of his comments about "honest graft" on his campaign. As newspaper reports about the book appeared, Plunkitt first declared flatly that "they know that I never stuck my hand out for graft." But once the book arrived and it was seen that Plunkitt was proud to admit he gained his fortune through graft— albeit allegedly "honest" graft—Plunkitt was forced to change his campaign tack. Now his claim was that he was being persecuted by his political opponents because he had never allowed "dirty" money into the district. "If I'd let this district be a bedhouse to satisfy some of the blackest scoundrels on earth I'd be all right. If I'd let the bootblacks and the peanut women be blackmailed $5 a month I'd be a good man. That's the only thing that can be brought up against me. If I'd allow filth and dirt here there wouldn't be nobody thinking he was making a run against old Plunkitt." While this claim was a clever attempt at political damage control, there is no way of knowing if it was true. And in any case Plunkitt's response could not stop the constant references to him in the press as "honest graft Plunkitt," or "the apostle of honest graft." Nor could he take back the book's boasts about his millions or his willingness to see his opportunities and take them.[60]

Four hundred police were assigned to the district on election day, and two calls for additional police help were put in during the day. More than fifty men were arrested on charges ranging from voting fraud to assault. At midnight Plunkitt and his allies conceded defeat and the supporters of McManus paraded through the district carrying a coffin symbolic of Plunkitt's political death. The next fall McManus completed his triumph by nominating himself for the state Senate seat that Plunkitt had held and winning that too. In 1907 Plunkitt made an attempt to retake the district leadership, but observers said from the start that his campaign was futile. The outcome was a three-thousand-vote slaughter that decisively ended the Plunkitt era.[61]

The election campaigns of 1904 and 1905 revealed yet another side of George Washington Plunkitt that was not much emphasized by Riordon. In these campaigns Plunkitt seemed arrogant, peevish, and obsessed with his millions. He claimed a sort of right to the leadership of his district because of his seniority and the money he had allegedly accumulated through his "honest" graft. Furthermore, his political vulnerability to the charges of "dishonest" graft (selling political nominations) and stinginess raised questions about whose benefit he had really worked for all those years and how much he actually did for the voters of his district. Was this stingy and dishonest man the real Plunkitt of Tammany Hall? Perhaps Plunkitt's career had followed the trajectory that Steffens proposed in 1903: from initial kindness to riches and power to "selling out" the residents of his district. Writing in the introduction to the 1948 edition of *Plunkitt of Tammany Hall,* political scientist Roy V. Peel said as much. Based on a study of Tammany ward bosses he had written in the 1930s, Peel wrote that the bosses lived a double life: "Once in the saddle [as a district leader] . . . you are selfish, cold, calculating, and corrupt but you maintain the illusion that you are generous, warm, informal, and honest. You deftly present one picture of yourself to your equals and still another to your superiors. You remain in power until times change and another younger man drives you into obscurity."[62]

READING *PLUNKITT OF TAMMANY HALL*

Media coverage of Plunkitt's death on November 19, 1924, revealed how well Riordon had done his job. By then George Washington Plunkitt and *Plunkitt of Tammany Hall* had almost become one. Plunkitt's humiliating political defeats of twenty years before were hardly mentioned, and Riordon's role in the composition of the book was almost ignored. Remembering Plunkitt as he was portrayed in the book, national magazines hailed him as a political sage while local newspapers speculated on the size of his estate, confidently predicting that it would add up into the millions. *The Nation,* then as now a leading voice of liberal opinion, declared that Plunkitt had been "one of the wisest men in American politics" and claimed that although he had been a "grafter," his constituents did not care because "they could understand a cheerful and honest grafter who made no pretense of virtue but did practical good right and left every day in the week."[63]

In reality Plunkitt was not a millionaire when he died, and he may never have been one. And there is considerable doubt about his status as a political wise man. When his estate was appraised one year after his death it contained only $280,000, mostly in real estate. While this was a substantial sum, it was surely a far cry from the millions with which he had tried to threaten his political opponents. Moreover, because prices had risen since 1905, it is possible that Plunkitt's holdings had been worth even less during his political heyday. Plunkitt's claim to be a millionaire—perhaps along with his claims of service and generosity—was part of the image he had created for himself. It was this image that his constituents had rejected in 1904 and 1905 when they showed they did care about his grafting by supporting candidates who claimed that Plunkitt had enriched himself at the expense of the district.[64]

Plunkitt of Tammany Hall remains a valuable historical source, however, even if everything it says about Tammany Hall in general and Plunkitt in particular is not true. This is so because it allows us to see how someone writing in 1905 could construct a portrayal of a ward boss that many people, both at the time and since then, have thought was true. One focus of our consideration of this book, then, should be on the author and what he used to construct such a portrayal in a particular context; another should be on the readers and how they read—and continue to read—the author's work. The readings in Part Two of this book have been selected to help us with these considerations because they come from the same time period.

As should be clear by now, *Plunkitt of Tammany Hall* is not simply reportage but a piece of persuasive or argumentative writing. Whether he or Plunkitt actually invented the famous phrases in the book, Riordon built the character of Plunkitt from a variety of sources. The first four and last two selections in Part Two are all other portrayals of Plunkitt in particular or ward bosses in general that appeared in print before this book. Which of these portrayals does Riordon appear to ignore? Which may have been sources for his portrait of Plunkitt? What do the answers to these questions tell us about who Riordon thought his audience was? How does his understanding of his audience differ from that of, say, the *Post*'s *Tammany Biographies*, *The Tammany Times*, Jane Addams, or Lincoln Steffens?

Riordon also selected, revised, and arranged the information in this book to make his points about Plunkitt and urban politics. What is the overall message that Riordon is trying to convey? Why does the book open with the section known as "Honest Graft and Dishonest Graft" and close with that entitled "Strenuous Life of the Tammany District Leader"? How does he highlight and repeat certain themes in the rest of the chapters? How do humor, satire, ridicule, and exaggeration help make his points? How does the concept of "honest" graft fit into his argument? How does Riordon's argument differ from that of Addams and Steffens? What techniques do Addams and Steffens use to make their points? Whose understanding of graft seems more persuasive, Riordon's or Steffens's?

In trying to answer these questions we join a long line of observers of the political machine whose understanding comes from *Plunkitt of Tammany Hall*. Three examples of direct responses to this book are in Part Two: two reviews of the 1905 edition of the book and *The Nation*'s 1924 discussion of Plunkitt's wisdom. How would you characterize the response of the reviewers? How does their tone compare with that of the article from *The Nation*?

Because we, too, are learning about the political machine from Plunkitt, we need to consider what experiences and references we bring to our own reading of the book. *The Nation* commended this book for "telling all that needs to be told about American politics," which was that "honesty doesn't matter, efficiency doesn't matter, progressive vision doesn't matter. What matters is the chance of a better job, a better price for wheat, better business conditions." Does this seem true about American politics then? Now? Would you like to live under a political machine? Why or why not? In general do you find yourself liking or disliking Plunkitt? Why? If you had to choose the portrayal of the political machine that most impressed you, would it be Riordon's, Addams's, or Steffens's? Why?[65]

A final way of thinking about the lasting value of this book is to consider less the "truth" it reveals and more the question it raises. Whatever else *Plunkitt of Tammany Hall* may have achieved or failed to achieve, it helped identify the parameters within which American politics has oscillated ever since. Published at the moment when the country first considered the appropriate role of the government in the economy, the book posed a crucial question. In Plunkitt's terms, can we build a society where everyone can "see his [or her] opportunities and take 'em" but where the less fortunate are also well provided for? *Plunkitt of Tammany Hall* argued that the machines had already found the answer to this question. But did they?

Have we?

NOTES

[1]For overviews of the social issues of the period, see Alan Trachtenberg, *The Incorporation of America: Culture and Society in the Gilded Age* (New York: Hill and Wang, 1982), and Nell Irvin Painter, *Standing at Armageddon: The United States, 1877–1919* (New York: Norton, 1989).

[2]Useful overviews of the political system in these years include Richard L. McCormick, *The Party Period and Public Policy* (New York: Oxford University Press, 1986); Stephen Skowronek, *Building a New American State: The Expansion of National Administrative Capacities, 1877–1920* (Cambridge: Cambridge University Press, 1982); and Morton Keller, *Affairs of State: Public Life in Late Nineteenth Century America* (Cambridge: Harvard University Press, 1977).

[3]The spectrum of debate over the parties can be seen in the works mentioned in notes 1 and 2 and also in Walter Dean Burnham, *Critical Elections and the Mainsprings of American Politics* (New York: Norton, 1970); Leon Fink, *Workingmen's Democracy: The Knights of Labor and American Politics* (Urbana: University of Illinois Press, 1983); Lawrence Goodwyn, *Democratic Promise: The Populist Moment in America* (New York: Oxford University Press, 1978); and Michael E. McGerr, *The Decline of Popular Politics: The American North, 1865–1928* (New York: Oxford University Press, 1986).

[4]M. J. Heale, *The Making of American Politics, 1750–1850* (London: Longman, 1977), is a useful, brief overview of the formation of the early American parties.

[5]Heale, *Making,* 158.

[6]Jon C. Teaford, *The Unheralded Triumph: City Government in America, 1870–1900* (Baltimore: Johns Hopkins University Press, 1984), surveys these city-building activities.

[7]For a classic discussion of the role of patronage and other incentives in machine politics, see Raymond Wolfinger, "Why Political Machines Have Not Withered Away and Other Revisionist Thoughts," *Journal of Politics* 34 (1972): 365–98. Recent works emphasizing the political machines' techniques of political control include Steven P. Erie, *Rainbow's End: Irish-Americans and the Dilemmas of Urban Machine Politics, 1840–1985* (Berkeley: University of California Press, 1988), and Martin Shefter, "The Emergence of the Political Machine: An Alternative View," in Willis Hawley et al., *Theoretical Perspectives on Urban Politics* (Englewood Cliffs: Prentice Hall, 1976). Erie examines the extent of patronage in New York and elsewhere. Not all ward bosses held public political office; some were party officials, and some held no formal political post at all.

[8]Harold Zink, *City Bosses in the United States: A Study of Twenty Municipal Bosses* (Durham: Duke University Press, 1930), 42–43, discusses the career patterns of bosses.

[9]New work on the timing, rise, and fall of political machines includes M. Craig Brown and Charles N. Halaby, "Machine Politics in America, 1870–1945," *Journal of Interdisciplinary History* 8 (1987): 587–612; Alan DiGaetano, "The Rise and Development of Urban Political Machines: An Alternative to Merton's Functional Analysis," *Urban Affairs Quarterly* 24 (1988):

242–67; Harvey Boulay and Alan DiGaetano, "Why Did Political Machines Disappear?," *Journal of Urban History* 12 (1985): 25–49.

[10] The effects of these changes on the political system are discussed in McCormick, *Party Period.*

[11] For accounts of Plunkitt's life and political career, see the articles in Part Two of this book in addition to "George Washington Plunkitt," *The New York Red Book: An Illustrated Legislative Manual* (New York, 1904); also see obituaries in the New York *Sun,* November 19, 1924; New York *Evening Post,* November 19, 1924; New York *World,* November 20, November 23, 1924; *New York Times,* November 29, 1924. All of these accounts seem influenced by the account in the *Red Book,* the text for which was undoubtedly provided by Plunkitt himself. For the census information about Plunkitt's family, see U.S. National Archives and Records Service, 7th Census of the United States, 1850 (Washington, D. C.: NARS, 1973), reel 559, 87.

[12] A useful history of both Tammany Halls is Alfred Connable and Edward Silberfarb, *Tigers of Tammany: Nine Men Who Ran New York* (New York: Rinehart and Winston, 1967).

[13] The standard account of New York City politics in Plunkitt's time is now David Hammack's *Power and Society: Greater New York at the Turn of the Century* (New York: Russell Sage Foundation, 1982).

[14] Useful accounts of the Tweed era include Amy Bridges, *A City in the Republic: Antebellum New York and the Origins of Machine Politics* (New York: Cambridge University Press, 1984); Jerome Mushkat, *Tammany: The Evolution of a Political Machine, 1789–1865* (Syracuse: Syracuse University Press, 1971); Alexander B. Callow, *The Tweed Ring* (New York: Oxford University Press, 1965); and Seymour J. Mandelbaum, *Boss Tweed's New York* (New York: Wiley, 1965).

[15] Alexander Callow describes the episode of the Young Democracy revolt against Tweed in *Tweed Ring,* 223–35.

[16] Hartley Davis, "Tammany Hall: The Most Perfect Political Organization in the World," *Munsey's,* October 1900, 58.

[17] Explanations of the structure of the Tammany Democracy can be found in the *New York Herald* Sunday magazine, September 17, 1905, and in Connable and Silberfarb, *Tigers,* 181–85. Martin Shefter emphasizes the importance of the district clubs in "The Emergence of the Political Machine: An Alternative View," in Willis Hawley, *Theoretical Perspectives.*

[18] Richard Croker, "Tammany Hall and the Democracy," *North American Review* 154 (1892): 225–30.

[19] The location of Plunkitt's homes can be followed in the *New York City Directory* (New York, 1865–1924). The following paragraphs on the area in which he lived are based on Pauline Goldmark, ed., *West Side Studies* (New York: Russell Sage Foundation, 1914), 2 vols. These volumes actually contain four separate studies of the area, including *Boyhood and Lawlessness,* and Ruth S. True, *The Neglected Girl,* in volume 1; and Ortho G. Cartwright, *The Middle West Side: A Historical Sketch,* and Katharine Anthony, *Mothers Who Must Earn,* in volume 2. Plunkitt himself was one of the sources for Cartwright's "sketch." Research for these studies was done in 1910, five years after Plunkitt left his post as Tammany District leader, but the studies focus on the lives of long-term residents of the area. Indeed, one of their most important findings was how many long-term residents there were. Therefore, they provide useful information on life in the district for the late nineteenth and early twentieth centuries. For a useful popular history of the same area, see Richard O'Connor, *Hell's Kitchen: The Roaring Days of New York's Wild West Side* (Philadelphia: Lippincott, 1958).

[20] Cartwright, *Middle West Side,* 33–42; Anthony, *Mothers,* 12–13.

[21] Anthony, *Mothers,* 2. Anthony's study was based on detailed employment histories of 370 working women and their husbands (if alive) that asked them to review their employment, wages, and so on, from their first job to 1910.

[22] Cartwright, *The Middle West Side,* 46–47. All the West Side studies remarked on the stability of the neighborhood. More than 60 percent of the families studied in *Boyhood and Lawlessness,* for example, had lived in the area fifteen years or more.

[23] *Boyhood and Lawlessness,* 1–5.

[24] For evidence of Plunkitt's church membership, see *New York Times,* November 23, November 25, 1924, and New York *Evening World,* November 9, 1904.

[25] Plunkitt is first listed at the West 51st Street address in the New York City Directory for 1891–92 and it is the same address given in his obituaries (note 11). The address of Washington Hall is given in many issues of *The Tammany Times.* See, for example, March 15, 1902, 7.

[26] For accounts of Plunkitt's day, see New York *Globe,* October 15, 1904; New York *World,* November 23, 1924; *New York Times Magazine,* February 1, 1925.

[27] *New York Times,* October 27, October 29, 1872, June 8, 1905; *New York Tribune,* August 5, 1894, October 12, 1903, January 30, 1906; New York *Evening Post,* October 17, 1903.

[28] Plunkitt's career in the Tammany Society can be followed in the "Membership List, 1789–1924" and "Minutes of the Grand Council of Sachems" of the Society of Tammany or Columbian Order in the City of New York, both in the Edwin P. Kilroe Collection of Tammaniana, Rare Book and Manuscript Library, Columbia University, New York.

[29] These parallels can only be suggestive. A full scale comparison of the organizations—taking into consideration their structures, ideologies, and rituals—remains to be done and would no doubt focus as much on the tensions within the organizations as on the power flowing down from the top of their hierarchies. For a recent overview of American Catholic historiography emphasizing the tensions within the church, see Leslie Woodcock Tentler, "On the Margins: The State of American Catholic History," *American Quarterly* 45 (1993): 104–27.

[30] Hammack, *Power and Society,* 158–85. For a useful account of the Henry George campaign against Tammany, see David Scobey, "Boycotting the Politics Factory: Labor Radicalism and the New York City Mayoral Election of 1886," *Radical History Review* 28–30 (1984): 280–325.

[31] *Boyhood and Lawlessness,* 70. Plunkitt's comments are from the sections of this book called "Ingratitude in Politics" and "Dangers of the Dress Suit in Politics."

[32] On rents, see Anthony, *Mothers,* 137. Juvenile fines are discussed in *Boyhood and Lawlessness,* 88.

[33] Anthony, *Mothers,* 89; *Boyhood and Lawlessness,* 88. Although undertaken by social workers, these studies were not intended to attack the ward bosses. The employed women and their husbands were asked the sources of all jobs they had held; the parents of juvenile delinquents were asked directly if they had ever received help from the boss. The latter study noted that those who had (or thought they had) "pull" with the boss liked to brag about it. This makes the few reports of aid even more credible.

[34] "Hon. Geo. W. Plunkitt," *Tammany Times,* September 21, 1895, 9; "George Washington Plunkitt," in *Tammany Biographies,* 3rd ed. (New York: Evening Post, 1894), 15–16. For the full text of these documents, see Part Two of this book.

[35] James Bryce, *The American Commonwealth* (London: Macmillan, 1888) 2:109. New York *Evening Post,* April 3, April 4, April 22, 1890.

[36] New York *Evening Post,* April 3, 1890.

[37] Hammack, *Power and Society,* 120.

[38] *The Tammany Times,* which called itself "a weekly newspaper devoted to the Tammany Organizations of the United States," began publication in 1892 and ceased publication sometime in the 1920s. The new history of Tammany was Euphemia Vale Blake, *History of the Tammany Society or Columbian Order from Its Organization to the Present Time* (New York: Souvenir Publishing, 1901).

[39] William T. Stead, "Mr. Richard Croker and Greater New York," *Review of Reviews* (London), October 17, 1897, 340–55.

[40] Hartley Davis, "Tammany Hall: The Most Perfect Political Organization in the World," *Munsey's,* October 1900; William Allen White, "Richard Croker," *McClure's,* October 1901, 317–26; Alfred Henry Lewis, *Richard Croker* (New York: Life, 1901).

[41] Jane Addams, "Why the Ward Boss Rules," *Outlook,* April 2, 1898; Lincoln Steffens, "New York: Good Government in Danger," *McClure's,* November 1903, 84–92. Both of these articles are reprinted in Part Two.

[42] For a useful biography of Addams that includes information on her Chicago activities, see

Allen F. Davis, *American Heroine* (New York: Oxford University Press, 1977). Addams's article was reprinted in two other places in 1898, and she used it extensively in later writings.

[43]Steffens's years on the *Post* are included in Justin Kaplan's *Lincoln Steffens: A Biography* (New York: Simon and Schuster, 1974).

[44]Steffens, "New York." This article was renamed "New York: Good Government to the Test" when the articles were published together in Steffens, *The Shame of the Cities* (New York: McClure, Phillips, 1904).

[45]Sources of this biographical information about Riordon are obituaries in *Editor and Publisher,* July 31, 1909; New York *Evening Post,* July 22, 1909; and *New York Times,* July 23, 1909.

[46]Allan Nevins, *The Evening Post: A Century of Journalism* (New York: Boni and Liveright, 1922), 550–51; *Editor and Publisher,* March 6, 1909.

[47]*New York Times,* July 23, 1909; New York *Evening Post,* July 22, 1909; Nevins, *The Evening Post,* 550.

[48]For examples of the Plunkitt interviews in the *Post,* see, for example, New York *Evening Post,* February 25, 1897; May 1, 1901; March 14, 1902; January 10, 1905.

[49]*The Journalist,* July 29, 1905; *Editor and Publisher,* July 31, 1909.

[50]John Seymour Wood, "Alfred Henry Lewis," *Bookman* 18 (January 1904): 486–94.

[51]For information on the circulation of *McClure's,* see Peter Lyon, *Success Story: The Life and Times of S. S. McClure* (New York: Scribner's, 1963), 251; Josiah Flynt, *The World of Graft* (New York: McClure, Phillips, 1901), 4.

[52]"The Reminiscences of Martin Saxe," Oral History Research Office, Columbia University, New York, 1948; New York *Globe,* October 15, 1904. Saxe's "Reminiscences" include both a microfilm copy of his papers and a transcribed oral history interview. For details of Saxe's biography, see "Testimonial Dinner to Honorable Martin Saxe," in "Reminiscences"; for reports of his work in the corporation counsel's office, see New York *Mail,* October 18, 1904; New York *Evening Post,* November 3, 1904.

[53]"Lift the Plunkitt Mortgage," election pamphlet, "Reminiscences"; New York *Evening Telegram,* November 3, 1904; New York *Sun,* October 23, 1904; New York *Evening Post,* November 3, 1904.

[54]New York *Globe,* October 15, 1904; New York *Evening Post,* November 10, 1904.

[55]*New York Times,* November 10, 1904; *New York Tribune,* October 30, 1904.

[56]New York *Sun,* November 10, 1904; New York *Evening Post,* November 9, 1904.

[57]*New York Times,* June 7, September 17, August 15, 1905.

[58]For accounts of the conservation, see New York *Evening Post,* June 7, 1905; *New York Times,* June 8, 1905. The latter is reprinted in Part Two of this book.

[59]New York *World,* September 2, September 3, 1905.

[60]New York *Sun,* September 3, 1905; New York *World,* September 6, 1905. For a useful recent look at the relationship between Tammany politicians and vice, see Timothy J. Gilfoyle, *City of Eros: New York City, Prostitution, and the Commercialization of Sex, 1790–1920* (New York: Norton, 1992).

[61]*New York Times,* September 20, 1905; New York *Evening Post,* September 20, 1905; New York *World,* September 25, 1907.

[62]Roy V. Peel, ed., *Plunkitt of Tammany Hall* (New York: Knopf, 1948), xvii–xviii. For a recent view of the image of another Tammany politician from Plunkitt's time, see Daniel Czitrom, "Underworlds and Underdogs: Big Tim Sullivan and Metropolitan Politics in New York, 1889–1913," *Journal of American History* 78 (1991): 536–59.

[63]"Plunkitt's Way," *The Nation,* December 3, 1924, 591.

[64]For a report on the valuation of Plunkitt's estate see *New York Times,* October 31, 1925.

[65]"Plunkitt's Way."

PART ONE

The Document

Plunkitt of Tammany Hall

A series of very plain talks on very
practical politics, delivered by ex-Senator
George Washington Plunkitt, the Tammany philosopher,
from his rostrum—the New York County court-house
bootblack stand—and recorded by
WILLIAM L. RIORDON

Preface

This volume discloses the mental operations of perhaps the most thoroughly practical politician of the day—George Washington Plunkitt, Tammany leader of the Fifteenth Assembly District, Sachem of the Tammany Society, and Chairman of the Elections Committee of Tammany Hall, who has held the offices of State Senator, Assemblyman, Police Magistrate, County Supervisor, and Alderman and who boasts of his record in filling four public offices in one year and drawing salaries from three of them at the same time.

The discourses that follow were delivered by him from his rostrum, the bootblack stand in the County Court-house, at various times in the last half-dozen years. Their absolute frankness and vigorous unconventionality of thought and expression charmed me. Plunkitt said right out what all practical politicians think but are afraid to say. Some of the discourses I published as interviews in the New York *Evening Post,* the New York *Sun,* the New York *World,* and the Boston *Transcript.* They were reproduced in newspapers throughout the country and several of them, notably the talks on "The Curse of Civil Service Reform" and "Honest Graft and Dishonest Graft," became subjects of discussion in the United States Senate and in college lectures. There seemed to be a general recognition of Plunkitt as a striking type of the practical politician, a politician, moreover, who dared to say publicly what others in his class whisper among themselves in the City Hall corridors and the hotel lobbies.

I thought it a pity to let Plunkitt's revelations of himself—as frank in their way as Rousseau's "Confessions"[1]—perish in the files of the newspapers; so I collected the talks I had published, added several new ones, and now give to the world in this volume a system of political philosophy which is as unique as it is refreshing.

No New Yorker needs to be informed who George Washington Plunkitt is. For the information of others, the following sketch of his career is given. He was born, as he proudly tells, in Central Park; that is, in the territory now included in the park. He began life as a driver of a cart, then became a butcher's boy, and later went into the butcher business for himself. How he entered politics he explains in one of his discourses. His advancement was rapid. He was in the Assembly soon after he cast his first vote and has held office most of the time for forty years. In 1870, through a strange combination of circumstances, he held the places of Assemblyman, Alderman, Police Magistrate, and County Supervisor and drew three salaries at once—a record unexampled in New York politics.

Plunkitt is now a millionaire. He owes his fortune mainly to his political pull, as he confesses in "Honest Graft and Dishonest Graft." The character of his business he also describes fully. He is in the contracting, transportation, real estate, and every other business out of which he can make money. He has no office. His headquarters is the County Court-house bootblack stand. There he receives his constituents, transacts his general business, and pours forth his philosophy.

Plunkitt has been one of the great powers in Tammany Hall, for a quarter of a century. While he was in the Assembly and the State Senate he was one of the most influential members and introduced the bills that provided for the outlying parks of New York City, the Harlem River Speedway, the Washington Bridge, the 155th Street Viaduct, the grading of Eighth Avenue north of Fifty-seventh Street, additions to the Museum of Natural History, the West Side Court, and many other important public improvements. He is one of the closest friends and most valued advisers of Charles F. Murphy, leader of Tammany Hall.

William L. Riordon

---

[1]Because of its purported frankness, philosopher Jean Jacques Rousseau's *Confessions* is thought by some literary critics to be the first modern autobiography. Although written in 1781, it was not widely available in English until the end of the nineteenth century.

Contents

Introduction

A Tribute to Plunkitt by the
Leader of Tammany Hall

Senator Plunkitt is a straight organization man. He believes in party government; he does not indulge in cant and hypocrisy and he is never afraid to say
exactly what he thinks. He is a believer in thorough political organization
and all-the-year-around work and he holds to the doctrine that, in making
appointments to office, party workers should be preferred if they are fitted
to perform the duties of the office. Plunkitt is one of the veteran leaders of
the organization, he has always been faithful and reliable, and he has
performed valuable services for Tammany Hall.

Charles F. Murphy

Plunkitt of
Tammany Hall

HONEST GRAFT AND
DISHONEST GRAFT

"Everybody is talkin' these days about Tammany men growin' rich on graft, but nobody thinks of drawin' the distinction between honest graft and dishonest graft. There's all the difference in the world between the two. Yes, many of our men have grown rich in politics. I have myself. I've made a big fortune out of the game, and I'm gettin' richer every day, but I've not gone in for dishonest graft—blackmailin' gamblers, saloon-keepers, disorderly people, etc.—and neither has any of the men who have made big fortunes in politics.

"There's an honest graft, and I'm an example of how it works. I might sum up the whole thing by sayin': 'I seen my opportunities and I took 'em.'

"Just let me explain by examples. My party's in power in the city, and it's goin' to undertake a lot of public improvements. Well, I'm tipped off, say, that they're going to lay out a new park at a certain place.

"I see my opportunity and I take it. I go to that place and I buy up all the land I can in the neighborhood. Then the board of this or that makes its plan public, and there is a rush to get my land, which nobody cared particular for before.

"Ain't it perfectly honest to charge a good price and make a profit on my investment and foresight? Of course, it is. Well, that's honest graft.

"Or, supposin' it's a new bridge they're goin' to build. I get tipped off and I buy as much property as I can that has to be taken for approaches. I sell at my own price later on and drop some more money in the bank.

"Wouldn't you? It's just like lookin' ahead in Wall Street or in the coffee or cotton market. It's honest graft, and I'm lookin' for it every day in the year. I will tell you frankly that I've got a good lot of it, too.

"I'll tell you of one case. They were goin' to fix up a big park, no matter where. I got on to it, and went lookin' about for land in that neighborhood.

"I could get nothin' at a bargain but a big piece of swamp, but I took it fast enough and held on to it. What turned out was just what I counted on. They couldn't make the park complete without Plunkitt's swamp, and they had to pay a good price for it. Anything dishonest in that?

"Up in the watershed I made some money, too. I bought up several bits of land there some years ago and made a pretty good guess that they would be bought up for water purposes later by the city.

"Somehow, I always guessed about right, and shouldn't I enjoy the profit of my foresight? It was rather amusin' when the condemnation commissioners came along and found piece after piece of the land in the name of George Plunkitt of the Fifteenth Assembly District, New York City. They wondered how I knew just what to buy. The answer is—I seen my opportunity and I took it. I haven't confined myself to land; anything that pays is in my line.

"For instance, the city is repavin' a street and has several hundred thousand old granite blocks to sell. I am on hand to buy, and I know just what they are worth.

"How? Never mind that. I had a sort of monopoly of this business for a while, but once a newspaper tried to do me. It got some outside men to come over from Brooklyn and New Jersey to bid against me.

"Was I done? Not much. I went to each of the men and said: 'How many of these 250,000 stones do you want?' One said 20,000, and another wanted 15,000, and another wanted 10,000. I said: 'All right, let me bid for the lot, and I'll give each of you all you want for nothin'.'

"They agreed, of course. Then the auctioneer yelled: 'How much am I bid for these 250,000 fine pavin' stones?'

" 'Two dollars and fifty cents,' says I.

" 'Two dollars and fifty cents!' screamed the auctioneer. 'Oh, that's a joke! Give me a real bid.'

"He found the bid was real enough. My rivals stood silent. I got the lot for $2.50 and gave them their share. That's how the attempt to do Plunkitt ended, and that's how all such attempts end.

"I've told you how I got rich by honest graft. Now, let me tell you that most politicians who are accused of robbin' the city get rich the same way.

"They didn't steal a dollar from the city treasury. They just seen their opportunities and took them. That is why, when a reform administration comes in and spends a half million dollars in tryin' to find the public robberies they talked about in the campaign, they don't find them.

"The books are always all right. The money in the city treasury is all right. Everything is all right. All they can show is that the Tammany heads of departments looked after their friends, within the law, and gave them what opportunities they could to make honest graft. Now, let me tell you that's never goin' to hurt Tammany with the people. Every good man looks after his friends, and any man who doesn't isn't likely to be popular. If I have a good thing to hand out in private life, I give it to a friend. Why shouldn't I do the same in public life?

"Another kind of honest graft. Tammany has raised a good many salaries. There was an awful howl by the reformers, but don't you know that Tammany gains ten votes for every one it lost by salary raisin'?

"The Wall Street banker thinks it shameful to raise a department clerk's salary from $1500 to $1800 a year, but every man who draws a salary himself says: 'That's all right. I wish it was me.' And he feels very much like votin' the Tammany ticket on election day, just out of sympathy.

"Tammany was beat in 1901 because the people were deceived into believin' that it worked dishonest graft. They didn't draw a distinction between dishonest and honest graft, but they saw that some Tammany men grew rich, and supposed they had been robbin' the city treasury or levyin' blackmail on disorderly houses, or workin' in with the gamblers and law-breakers.

"As a matter of policy, if nothing else, why should the Tammany leaders go into such dirty business, when there is so much honest graft lyin' around when they are in power? Did you ever consider that?

"Now, in conclusion, I want to say that I don't own a dishonest dollar. If my worst enemy was given the job of writin' my epitaph when I'm gone, he couldn't do more than write:

" 'George W. Plunkitt. He Seen His Opportunities, and He Took 'Em.' "

HOW TO BECOME A STATESMAN

"There's thousands of young men in this city who will go to the polls for the first time next November. Among them will be many who have watched the careers of successful men in politics, and who are longin' to make names and fortunes for themselves at the same game. It is to these youths that I want to give advice. First, let me say that I am in a position to give what the courts call expert testimony on the subject. I don't think you can easily find a better example than I am of success in politics. After forty years' experience at the game I am—well, I'm George Washington Plunkitt. Everybody knows what figure I cut in the greatest organization on earth, and if you hear people say that I've laid away a million or so since I was a butcher's boy in Washington Market, don't come to me for an indignant denial. I'm pretty comfortable, thank you.

"Now, havin' qualified as an expert, as the lawyers say, I am goin' to give advice free to the young men who are goin' to cast their first votes, and who are lookin' forward to political glory and lots of cash. Some young men think they can learn how to be successful in politics from books, and they cram their heads with all sorts of college rot. They couldn't make a bigger mistake. Now, understand me, I ain't sayin' nothin' against colleges. I guess they'll have to exist as long as there's bookworms, and I suppose they do some good in a certain way, but they don't count in politics. In fact, a young man who has gone through the college course is handicapped at the outset. He may succeed in politics, but the chances are 100 to 1 against him.

"Another mistake; some young men think that the best way to prepare for the political game is to practise speakin' and becomin' orators. That's all wrong. We've got some orators in Tammany Hall, but they're chiefly ornamental. You never heard of Charlie Murphy delivering a speech, did you? Or Richard Croker, or John Kelly, or any other man who has been a real power in the organization? Look at the thirty-six district leaders of Tammany Hall to-day. How many of them travel on their tongues? Maybe one or two, and they don't count when business is doin' at Tammany Hall. The men who rule have practised keepin' their tongues still, not exercisin' them. So you want to drop the orator idea unless you mean to go into politics just to perform the sky-rocket act.

"Now, I've told you what not to do; I guess I can explain best what to do to succeed in politics by tellin' you what I did. After goin' through the apprenticeship of the business while I was a boy by workin' around the district headquarters and hustlin' about the polls on election day, I set out when I cast my first vote to win fame and money in New York city politics. Did I offer my services to the district leader as a stump-speaker? Not much. The woods are always full of speakers. Did I get up a book on municipal government and show it to the leader? I wasn't such a fool. What I did was to get some marketable goods before goin' to the leaders. What do I mean by marketable goods? Let me tell you: I had a cousin, a young man who didn't take any particular interest in politics. I went to him and said: 'Tommy, I'm goin' to be a politician, and I want to get a followin'; can I count on you?' He said: 'Sure, George.' That's how I started in business. I got a marketable commodity—one vote. Then I went to the district leader and told him I could command two votes on election day, Tommy's and my own. He smiled on me and told me to go ahead. If I had offered him a speech or a bookful of learnin', he would have said, 'Oh, forget it!'

"That was beginnin' business in a small way, wasn't it? But that is the only way to become a real lastin' statesman. I soon branched out. Two young men in the flat next to mine were school friends. I went to them, just as I went to Tommy, and they agreed to stand by me. Then I had a followin' of three voters and I began to get a bit chesty. Whenever I dropped into district headquarters, everybody shook hands with me, and the leader one day honored me by lightin' a match for my cigar. And so it went on like a snowball rollin' down a hill. I worked the flat-house that I lived in from the basement to the top floor, and I got about a dozen young men to follow me. Then I tackled the next house and so on down the block and around the corner. Before long I had sixty men back of me, and formed the George Washington Plunkitt Association.

"What did the district leader say then when I called at headquarters? I didn't have to call at headquarters. He came after me and said: 'George, what do you want? If you don't see what you want, ask for it. Wouldn't you like to have a job or two in the departments for your friends?' I said: 'I'll think it over; I haven't yet decided what the George Washington Plunkitt Association will do in the next campaign.' You ought to have seen how I was courted and petted then by the leaders of the rival organizations. I had marketable goods and there was bids for them from all sides, and I was a risin' man in politics. As time went on, and my association grew, I thought I would like to go to the Assembly. I just had to hint at what I wanted, and three different organizations offered me the nomination. Afterwards, I went to the Board of Aldermen, then to the State Senate, then became leader of the district, and so on up and up till I became a statesman.

"That is the way and the only way to make a lastin' success in politics. If you are goin' to cast your first vote next November and want to go into politics, do as I did. Get a followin', if it's only one man, and then go to the district leader and say: 'I want to join the organization. I've got one man who'll follow me through thick and thin.' The leader won't laugh at your one-man followin'. He'll shake your hand warmly, offer to propose you for membership in his club, take you down to the corner for a drink, and ask you to call again. But go to him and say: 'I took first prize at college in Aristotle; I can recite all Shakspere forwards and backwards; there ain't nothin' in science that ain't as familiar to me as blockades on the elevated roads and I'm the real thing in the way of silver-tongued orators.' What will he answer? He'll probably say: 'I guess you are not to blame for your misfortunes, but we have no use for you here.' "

THE CURSE OF
CIVIL SERVICE REFORM

"This civil service law is the biggest fraud of the age. It is the curse of the nation. There can't be no real patriotism while it lasts. How are you goin' to interest our young men in their country if you have no offices to give them when they work for their party? Just look at things in this city to-day. There are ten thousand good offices, but we can't get at more than a few hundred of them. How are we goin' to provide for the thousands of men who worked for the Tammany ticket? It can't be done. These men were full of patriotism a short time ago. They expected to be servin' their city, but when we tell them that we can't place them, do you think their patriotism is goin' to last? Not much. They say: 'What's the use of workin' for your country anyhow? There's nothin' in the game.' And what can they do? I don't know, but I'll tell you what I do know. I know more than one young man in past years who worked for the ticket and was just overflowin' with patriotism, but when he was knocked out by the civil service humbug he got to hate his country and became an Anarchist.

"This ain't no exaggeration. I have good reason for sayin' that most of the Anarchists in this city to-day are men who ran up against civil service examinations. Isn't it enough to make a man sour on his country when he wants to serve it and won't be allowed unless he answers a lot of fool questions about the number of cubic inches of water in the Atlantic and the quality of sand in the Sahara desert? There was once a bright young man in my district who tackled one of these examinations. The next I heard of him he had settled down in Herr Most's saloon smokin' and drinkin' beer and talkin' socialism all day. Before that time he had never drank anything but whisky. I knew what was comin' when a young Irishman drops whisky and takes to beer and long pipes in a German saloon. That young man is to-day one of the wildest Anarchists in town. And just to think! He might be a patriot but for that cussed civil service.

"Say, did you hear about that Civil Service Reform Association kickin' because the tax commissioners want to put their fifty-five deputies on the exempt list, and fire the outfit left to them by Low? That's civil service for you. Just think! Fifty-five Republicans and mugwumps[2] holdin' $3000 and $4000 and $5000 jobs in the tax department when 1555 good Tammany men are ready and willin' to take their places! It's an outrage! What did the people

[2]Republicans fed up with the power of the spoils system in that party who voted for Democrat Grover Cleveland for president in 1884 were called "mugwumps," and this word later came to stand for reformers, especially those who seemed pompous or self-important. New York *Evening Post* editor E. L. Godkin was a prominent mugwump.

mean when they voted for Tammany. What is representative government, anyhow? Is it all a fake that this is a government of the people, by the people, and for the people? If it isn't a fake, then why isn't the people's voice obeyed and Tammany men put in all the offices?

"When the people elected Tammany, they knew just what they were doin'. We didn't put up any false pretences. We didn't go in for humbug civil service and all that rot. We stood as we have always stood, for rewardin' the men that won the victory. They call that the spoils system. All right; Tammany is for the spoils system, and when we go in we fire every anti-Tammany man from office that can be fired under the law. It's an elastic sort of law and you can bet it will be stretched to the limit. Of course the Republican State Civil Service Board will stand in the way of our local Civil Service Commission all it can; but say!—suppose we carry the State some time won't we fire the up-State[3] Board all right? Or we'll make it work in harmony with the local board, and that means that Tammany will get everything in sight. I know that the civil service humbug is stuck into the constitution, too, but, as Tim Campbell said: 'What's the constitution among friends?'

"Say, the people's voice is smothered by the cursed civil service law; it is the root of all evil in our government. You hear of this thing or that thing goin' wrong in the nation, the State, or the city. Look down beneath the surface and you can trace everything wrong to civil service. I have studied the subject and I know. The civil service humbug is underminin' our institutions and if a halt ain't called soon this great republic will tumble down like a Park-avenue house when they were buildin' the subway, and on its ruins will rise another Russian government.

"This is an awful serious proposition. Free silver and the tariff and imperialism and the Panama Canal are triflin' issues when compared to it. We could worry along without any of these things, but civil service is sappin' the foundation of the whole shootin' match. Let me argue it out for you. I ain't up on sillygisms,[4] but I can give you some arguments that nobody can answer.

"First this great and glorious country was built up by political parties; second, parties can't hold together if their workers don't get the offices when they win; third, if the parties go to pieces, the government they built up must go to pieces, too; fourth, then there'll be h—— to pay.

"Could anything be clearer than that? Say, honest now; can you answer

---

[3]In Plunkitt's mind just about everything outside of metropolitan New York City was "upstate," but this distinction refers more properly to the perceived conflict between the state legislature (upstate in Albany) and New York City.

[4]Pun on *syllogism,* a formal argument.

that argument? Of course you won't deny that the government was built up by the great parties. That's history, and you can't go back of the returns. As to my second proposition, you can't deny that either. When parties can't get offices, they'll bust. They ain't far from the bustin' point now, with all this civil service business keepin' most of the good things from them. How are you goin' to keep up patriotism if this thing goes on? You can't do it. Let me tell you that patriotism has been dying out fast for the last twenty years. Before then when a party won, its workers got everything in sight. That was somethin' to make a man patriotic. Now, when a party wins and its men come forward and ask for their reward, the reply is, 'Nothin' doin', unless you can answer a list of questions about Egyptian mummies and how many years it will take for a bird to wear out a mass of iron as big as the earth by steppin' on it once in a century?'

"I have studied politics and men for forty-five years, and I see how things are driftin'. Sad indeed is the change that has come over the young men, even in my district, where I try to keep up the fire of patriotism by gettin' a lot of jobs for my constituents, whether Tammany is in or out. The boys and men don't get excited any more when they see a United States flag or hear the 'Star Spangled Banner.' They don't care no more for fire-crackers on the Fourth of July. And why should they? What is there in it for them? They know that no matter how hard they work for their country in a campaign, the jobs will go to fellows who can tell about the mummies and the bird steppin' on the iron. Are you surprised then that the young men of the country are beginnin' to look coldly on the flag and don't care to put up a nickel for fire-crackers?

"Say, let me tell of one case. After the battle of San Juan Hill,[5] the Americans found a dead man with a light complexion, red hair, and blue eyes. They could see he wasn't a Spaniard, although he had on a Spanish uniform. Several officers looked him over, and then a private of the Seventy-first Regiment saw him and yelled, 'Good Lord, that's Flaherty.' That man grew up in my district, and he was once the most patriotic American boy on the West Side. He couldn't see a flag without yellin' himself hoarse.

"Now, how did he come to be lying dead with a Spanish uniform on? I found out all about it, and I'll vouch for the story. Well, in the municipal campaign of 1897, that young man, chockful of patriotism, worked day and night for the Tammany ticket. Tammany won, and the young man determined to devote his life to the service of the city. He picked out a place that would suit him, and sent in his application to the head of department. He got

[5]A major battle—fought outside Santiago, Cuba, on July 1, 1898—in the Spanish-American War.

a reply that he must take a civil service examination to get the place. He didn't know what these examinations were, so he went, all light-hearted, to the Civil Service Board. He read the questions about the mummies, the bird on the iron, and all the other fool questions—and he left that office an enemy of the country that he had loved so well. The mummies and the bird blasted his patriotism. He went to Cuba, enlisted in the Spanish army at the breakin' out of the war, and died fightin' his country.

"That is but one victim of the infamous civil service. If that young man had not run up against the civil examination, but had been allowed to serve his country as he wished, he would be in a good office to-day, drawin' a good salary. Ah, how many young men have had their patriotism blasted in the same way!

"Now, what is goin' to happen when civil service crushes out patriotism? Only one thing can happen—the republic will go to pieces. Then a czar or a sultan will turn up, which brings me to the fourthly of my argument; that is, there will be h—— to pay. And that ain't no lie."

REFORMERS ONLY MORNIN' GLORIES

"College professors and philosophers who go up in a balloon to think are always discussin' the question: 'Why Reform Administrations Never Succeed Themselves!' The reason is plain to anybody who has learned the a, b, c of politics.

"I can't tell just how many of these movements I've seen started in New York during my forty years in politics, but I can tell you how many have lasted more than a few years—none. There have been reform committees of fifty, of sixty, of seventy, of one hundred, and all sorts of numbers that started out to do up the regular political organizations. They were mornin' glories—looked lovely in the mornin' and withered up in a short time, while the regular machines went on flourishin' forever, like fine old oaks. Say, that's the first poetry I ever worked off. Ain't it great?

"Just look back a few years. You remember the People's Municipal League that nominated Frank Scott for mayor in 1890? Do you remember the reformers that got up that league? Have you ever heard of them since? I haven't. Scott himself survived because he had always been a first-rate politician, but you'd have to look in the newspaper almanacs of 1891 to find out who made up the People's Municipal League. Oh, yes! I remember one name—Ollie Teall; dear, pretty Ollie and his big dog. They're about all that's left of the League.

"Now take the reform movement of 1894. A lot of good politicians joined in that—the Republicans, the State Democrats, the Stecklerites, and the O'Brienites, and they gave us a lickin', but the real reform part of the affair, the Committee of Seventy[6] that started the thing goin', what's become of those reformers? What's become of Charles Stewart Smith? Where's Bangs? Do you ever hear of Cornell, the iron man, in politics now? Could a search party find R. W. G. Welling? Have you seen the name of Fulton McMahon or McMahon Fulton—I ain't sure which—in the papers lately? Or Preble Tucker? Or—but it's no use to go through the list of the reformers who said they sounded in the death knell of Tammany in 1894. They're gone for good, and Tammany's pretty well, thank you. They did the talkin' and posin', and the politicians in the movement got all the plums. It's always the case.

"The Citizens' Union has lasted a little bit longer than the reform crowd that went before them, but that's because they learned a thing or two from us. They learned how to put up a pretty good bluff—and bluff counts a lot in politics. With only a few thousand members, they had the nerve to run the whole Fusion movement,[7] make the Republicans and other organizations come to their headquarters to select a ticket and dictate what every candidate must do or not do. I love nerve, and I've had a sort of respect for the Citizens' Union lately, but the Union can't last. Its people haven't been trained to politics, and whenever Tammany calls their bluff they lay right down. You'll never hear of the Union again after a year or two.

"And, by the way, what's become of the good government clubs, the political nurseries of a few years ago? Do you ever hear of Good Government Club D and P and Q and Z any more? What's become of the infants who were to grow up and show us how to govern the city? I know what's become of the nursery that was started in my district. You can find pretty much the whole outfit over in my headquarters, Washington Hall.

"The fact is that a reformer can't last in politics. He can make a show for a while, but he always comes down like a rocket. Politics is as much a regular business as the grocery or the dry-goods or the drug business. You've got to be trained up to it or you're sure to fall. Suppose a man who knew nothing about the grocery trade suddenly went into the business and tried to conduct it according to his own ideas. Wouldn't he make a mess of it? He might make a splurge for a while, as long as his money lasted, but his store would soon

---

[6]The Committee of Seventy sponsored William L. Strong's successful campaign for mayor of New York City in 1894. Supporters of the campaign included both reformers and disgruntled members of Tammany called Stecklerites and O'Brienites after the leaders of their factions.

[7]The Fusion movement refers to the effort of Tammany's political opponents of various stripes (Republicans, disgruntled Democrats, independents) to come together (fuse) and support the same candidates for municipal office. Such campaigns placed candidates on the ballot (under a variety of names) regularly after 1890. Both William L. Strong and Seth Low were elected mayor because of fusion activity.

be empty. It's just the same with a reformer. He hasn't been brought up in the difficult business of politics and he makes a mess of it every time.

"I've been studyin' the political game for forty-five years, and I don't know it all yet. I'm learnin' somethin' all the time. How, then, can you expect what they call 'business men' to turn into politics all at once and make a success of it? It is just as if I went up to Columbia University and started to teach Greek. They usually last about as long in politics as I would last at Columbia.

"You can't begin too early in politics if you want to succeed at the game. I began several years before I could vote, and so did every successful leader in Tammany Hall. When I was twelve years old I made myself useful around the district headquarters and did work at all the polls on election day. Later on, I hustled about gettin' out voters who had jags on or who were too lazy to come to the polls. There's a hundred ways that boys can help, and they get an experience that's the first real step in statesmanship. Show me a boy that hustles for the organization on election day, and I'll show you a comin' statesman.

"That's the a b c of politics. It ain't easy work to get up to y and z. You have to give nearly all your time and attention to it. Of course, you may have some business or occupation on the side, but the great business of your life must be politics if you want to succeed in it. A few years ago Tammany tried to mix politics and business in equal quantities, by havin' two leaders for each district, a politician and a business man. They wouldn't mix. They were like oil and water. The politician looked after the politics of his district; the business man looked after his grocery store or his milk route, and whenever he appeared at an executive meeting, it was only to make trouble. The whole scheme turned out to be a farce and was abandoned mighty quick.

"Do you understand now, why it is that a reformer goes down and out in the first or second round, while a politician answers to the gong every time? It is because the one has gone into the fight without trainin', while the other trains all the time and knows every fine point of the game."

NEW YORK CITY IS PIE FOR THE HAYSEEDS

"This city is ruled entirely by the hayseed legislators at Albany. I've never known an up-State Republican who didn't want to run things here, and I've met many thousands of them in my long service in the Legislature. The hayseeds think we are like the Indians to the National Government—that is, sort of wards of the State, who don't know how to look after ourselves and have to be taken care of by the Republicans of St. Lawrence, Ontario, and other backwoods counties. Why should anybody be surprised because ex-Governor Odell comes down here to direct the Republican machine? Newburg ain't big enough for him. He, like all the other up-State Republicans, wants to get hold of New York City. New York is their pie.

"Say, you hear a lot about the downtrodden people of Ireland and the Russian peasants and the sufferin' Boers. Now, let me tell you that they have more real freedom and home rule than the people of this grand and imperial city.[8] In England, for example, they make a pretense of givin' the Irish some self-government. In this State the Republican government makes no pretense at all. It says right out in the open: 'New York City is a nice big fat Goose. Come along with your carvin' knives and have a slice.' They don't pretend to ask the Goose's consent.

"We don't own our streets or our docks or our water front or anything else. The Republican Legislature and Governor run the whole shootin'-match. We've got to eat and drink what they tell us to eat and drink, and have got to choose our time for eatin' and drinkin' to suit them. If they don't feel like takin' a glass of beer on Sunday, we must abstain. If they have not got any amusements up in their backwoods, we mustn't have none. We've got to regulate our whole lives to suit them. And then we have to pay their taxes to boot.

"Did you ever go up to Albany from this city with a delegation that wanted anything from the Legislature? No? Well, don't. The hayseeds who run all the committees will look at you as if you were a child that didn't know what it wanted, and will tell you in so many words to go home and be good and the Legislature will give you whatever it thinks is good for you. They put on a sort of patronizing air, as much as to say, 'These children are an awful lot of trouble. They're wantin' candy all the time, and they know that it will make them sick. They ought to thank goodness that they have us to take care of them.' And if you try to argue with them, they'll smile in a pityin' sort of way as if they were humorin' a spoiled child.

"But just let a Republican farmer from Chemung or Wayne or Tioga turn up at the Capital. The Republican Legislature will make a rush for him and ask him what he wants and tell him if he doesn't see what he wants to ask

---

[8]The home rule movement in America removed cities from the jurisdiction of state legislatures, thus making local governments the last word on municipal legislation. Plunkitt exaggerates New York's situation by comparing it with that of the Irish, who had long sought independence from England; the Boers, descendants of Dutch settlers in South Africa, who had fought a losing war for independence from Britain from 1899 to 1902; and Russian peasants, thought by Americans to be oppressed by the Russian czar.

for it. If he says his taxes are too high, they reply to him: 'All right, old man, don't let that worry you. How much do you want us to take off?'

" 'I guess about fifty per cent will about do for the present,' says the man. 'Can you fix me up?'

" 'Sure,' the Legislature agrees. 'Give us somethin' harder, don't be bashful. We'll take off sixty per cent if you wish. That's what we're here for.'

"Then the Legislature goes and passes a law increasin' the liquor tax or some other tax in New York City, takes a half of the proceeds for the State Treasury and cuts down the farmers' taxes to suit. It's as easy as rollin' off a log—when you've got a good workin' majority and no conscience to speak of.

"Let me give you another example. It makes me hot under the collar to tell about this. Last year some hayseeds along the Hudson River, mostly in Odell's neighborhood, got dissatisfied with the docks where they landed their vegetables, brickbats, and other things they produce in the river counties. They got together and said: 'Let's take a trip down to New York and pick out the finest dock we can find. Odell and the Legislature will do the rest.' They did come down here, and what do you think they hit on? The finest dock in my district. Invaded George W. Plunkitt's district without sayin' as much as 'by your leave.' Then they called on Odell to put through a bill givin' them this dock, and he did.

"When the bill came before Mayor Low I made the greatest speech of my life. I pointed out how the Legislature could give the whole water front to the hayseeds over the head of the Dock Commissioner in the same way, and warned the Mayor that nations had rebelled against their governments for less. But it was no go. Odell and Low were pards[9] and—well, my dock was stolen.

"You heard a lot in the State campaign about Odell's great work in reducin' the State tax to almost nothin', and you'll hear a lot more about it in the campaign next year. How did he do it? By cuttin' down the expenses of the State Government? Oh, no! The expenses went up. He simply performed the old Republican act of milkin' New York City. The only difference was that he nearly milked the city dry. He not only ran up the liquor tax, but put all sorts of taxes on corporations, banks, insurance companies, and everything in sight that could be made to give up. Of course, nearly the whole tax fell on the city. Then Odell went through the country districts and said: 'See what I have done for you. You ain't got any more taxes to pay the State. Ain't I a fine feller?'

"Once a farmer in Orange County asked him: 'How did you do it, Ben?'

---

[9]Partners.

" 'Dead easy,' he answered. 'Whenever I want any money for the State Treasury, I know where to get it,' and he pointed toward New York City.

"And then all the Republican tinkerin' with New York City's charter. Nobody can keep up with it. When a Republican mayor is in, they give him all sorts of power. If a Tammany mayor is elected next fall I wouldn't be surprised if they changed the whole business and arranged it so that every city department should have four heads, two of them Republicans. If we made a kick, they would say: 'You don't know what's good for you. Leave it to us. It's our business.' "

TO HOLD YOUR DISTRICT—
STUDY HUMAN NATURE
AND ACT ACCORDIN'

"There's only one way to hold a district; you must study human nature and act accordin'. You can't study human nature in books. Books is a hindrance more than anything else. If you have been to college, so much the worse for you. You'll have to unlearn all you learned before you can get right down to human nature, and unlearnin' takes a lot of time. Some men can never forget what they learned at college. Such men may get to be district leaders by a fluke, but they never last.

"To learn real human nature you have to go among the people, see them and be seen. I know every man, woman, and child in the Fifteenth District, except them that's been born this summer—and I know some of them, too. I know what they like and what they don't like, what they are strong at and what they are weak in, and I reach them by approachin' at the right side.

"For instance, here's how I gather in the young men. I hear of a young feller that's proud of his voice, thinks that he can sing fine. I ask him to come around to Washington Hall and join our Glee Club. He comes and sings, and he's a follower of Plunkitt for life. Another young feller gains a reputation as a base-ball player in a vacant lot. I bring him into our base-ball club. That fixes him. You'll find him workin' for my ticket at the polls next election day. Then there's the feller that likes rowin' on the river, the young feller that makes a name as a waltzer on his block, the young feller that's handy with his dukes—I rope them all in by givin' them opportunities to show themselves off. I don't trouble them with political arguments. I just study human nature and act accordin'.

"But you may say this game won't work with the high-toned fellers, the fellers that go through college and then join the Citizens' Union. Of course it wouldn't work. I have a special treatment for them. I ain't like the patent medicine man that gives the same medicine for all diseases. The Citizens' Union kind of a young man! I love him! He's the daintiest morsel of the lot, and he don't often escape me.

"Before telling you how I catch him, let me mention that before the election last year, the Citizens' Union said they had four hundred or five hundred enrolled voters in my district. They had a lovely headquarters, too, beautiful roll-top desks and the cutest rugs in the world. If I was accused of havin' contributed to fix up the nest for them, I wouldn't deny it under oath. What do I mean by that? Never mind. You can guess from the sequel, if you're sharp.

"Well, election day came. The Citizens' Union's candidate for Senator, who ran against me, just polled five votes in the district, while I polled something more than 14,000 votes. What became of the 400 or 500 Citizens' Union enrolled voters in my district? Some people guessed that many of them were good Plunkitt men all along and worked with the Cits just to bring them into the Plunkitt camp by election day. You can guess that way, too, if you want to. I never contradict stories about me, especially in hot weather. I just call your attention to the fact that on last election day 395 Citizens' Union enrolled voters in my district were missin' and unaccounted for.

"I tell you frankly, though, how I have captured some of the Citizens' Union's young men. I have a plan that never fails. I watch the City Record to see when there's civil service examinations for good things. Then I take my young Cit in hand, tell him all about the good thing and get him worked up till he goes and takes an examination. I don't bother about him any more. It's a cinch that he comes back to me in a few days and asks to join Tammany Hall. Come over to Washington Hall some night and I'll show you a list of names on our rolls marked 'C. S.' which means, 'bucked up against civil service.'

"As to the older voters, I reach them, too. No, I don't send them campaign literature. That's rot. People can get all the political stuff they want to read—and a good deal more, too—in the papers. Who reads speeches, nowadays, anyhow? It's bad enough to listen to them. You ain't goin' to gain any votes by stuffin' the letter boxes with campaign documents. Like as not you'll lose votes, for there's nothin' a man hates more than to hear the letter-carrier ring his bell and go to the letter-box expectin' to find a letter he was lookin' for, and find only a lot of printed politics. I met a man this very mornin' who told me he voted the Democratic State ticket last year just because the Republicans kept crammin' his letter-box with campaign documents.

"What tells in holdin' your grip on your district is to go right down among the poor families and help them in the different ways they need help. I've got a regular system for this. If there's a fire in Ninth, Tenth, or Eleventh Avenue, for example, any hour of the day or night, I'm usually there with some of my election district captains as soon as the fire-engines. If a family is burned out I don't ask whether they are Republicans or Democrats, and I don't refer them to the Charity Organization Society, which would investigate their case in a month or two and decide they were worthy of help about the time they are dead from starvation. I just get quarters for them, buy clothes for them if their clothes were burned up, and fix them up till they get things runnin' again. It's philanthropy, but it's politics, too—mighty good politics. Who can tell how many votes one of these fires bring me? The poor are the most grateful people in the world, and, let me tell you, they have more friends in their neighborhoods than the rich have in theirs.

"If there's a family in my district in want I know it before the charitable societies do, and me and my men are first on the ground. I have a special corps to look up such cases. The consequence is that the poor look up to George W. Plunkitt as a father, come to him in trouble—and don't forget him on election day.

"Another thing, I can always get a job for a deservin' man. I make it a point to keep on the track of jobs, and it seldom happens that I don't have a few up my sleeve ready for use. I know every big employer in the district and in the whole city, for that matter, and they ain't in the habit of sayin' no to me when I ask them for a job.

"And the children—the little roses of the district! Do I forget them? Oh, no! They know me, every one of them, and they know that a sight of Uncle George and candy means the same thing. Some of them are the best kind of vote-getters. I'll tell you a case. Last year a little Eleventh Avenue rosebud whose father is a Republican, caught hold of his whiskers on election day and said she wouldn't let go till he'd promise to vote for me. And she didn't."

ON "THE SHAME OF THE CITIES"

"I've been readin' a book by Lincoln Steffens on 'The Shame of the Cities.' Steffens means well but, like all reformers, he don't know how to make distinctions. He can't see no difference between honest graft and dishonest graft and, consequent, he gets things all mixed up. There's the biggest kind of a difference between political looters and politicians who make a fortune out of politics by keepin' their eyes wide open. The looter goes in for himself alone without considerin' his organization or his city. The politician looks after his own interests, the organization's interests, and the city's interests all at the same time. See the distinction? For instance, I ain't no looter. The looter hogs it. I never hogged. I made my pile in politics, but, at the same time, I served the organization and got more big improvements for New York City than any other livin' man. And I never monkeyed with the penal code.

"The difference between a looter and a practical politician is the difference between the Philadelphia Republican gang and Tammany Hall. Steffens seems to think they're both about the same; but he's all wrong. The Philadelphia crowd runs up against the penal code. Tammany don't. The Philadelphians ain't satisfied with robbin' the bank of all its gold and paper money. They stay to pick up the nickels and pennies and the cop comes and nabs them. Tammany ain't no such fool. Why, I remember, about fifteen or twenty years ago, a Republican superintendent of the Philadelphia almshouse stole the zinc roof off the buildin' and sold it for junk. That was carryin' things to excess. There's a limit to everything, and the Philadelphia Republicans go beyond the limit. It seems like they can't be cool and moderate like real politicians. It ain't fair, therefore, to class Tammany men with the Philadelphia gang. Any man who undertakes to write political books should never for a moment lose sight of the distinction between honest graft and dishonest graft, which I explained in full in another talk. If he puts all kinds of graft on the same level, he'll make the fatal mistake that Steffens made and spoil his book.

"A big city like New York or Philadelphia or Chicago might be compared to a sort of Garden of Eden, from a political point of view. It's an orchard full of beautiful apple-trees. One of them has got a big sign on it, marked: 'Penal Code Tree—Poison.' The other trees have lots of apples on them for all. Yet, the fools go to the Penal Code Tree. Why? For the reason, I guess, that a cranky child refuses to eat good food and chews up a box of matches with relish. I never had any temptation to touch the Penal Code Tree. The other apples are good enough for me, and O Lord! how many of them there are in a big city!

"Steffens made one good point in his book. He said he found that Philadelphia, ruled almost entirely by Americans, was more corrupt than New York, where the Irish do almost all the governin'. I could have told him that before he did any investigatin' if he had come to me. The Irish was born to rule, and they're the honestest people in the world. Show me the Irishman who would steal a roof off an almshouse! He don't exist. Of course, if an Irishman had the political pull and the roof was much worn, he might get the city authorities to put on a new one and get the contract for it himself, and buy the old roof at a bargain—but that's honest graft. It's goin' about the thing like a gentleman—and there's more money in it than in tearin' down an old roof and cartin' it to the junkman's—more money and no penal code.

"One reason why the Irishman is more honest in politics than many Sons of the Revolution is that he is grateful to the country and the city that gave him protection and prosperity when he was driven by oppression from the Emerald Isle. Say, that sentence is fine, ain't it? I'm goin' to get some literary feller to work it over into poetry for next St. Patrick's Day dinner.

"Yes, the Irishman is grateful. His one thought is to serve the city which gave him a home. He has this thought even before he lands in New York, for his friends here often have a good place in one of the city departments picked out for him while he is still in the old country. Is it any wonder that he has a tender spot in his heart for old New York when he is on its salary list the mornin' after he lands?

"Now, a few words on the general subject of the so-called shame of cities. I don't believe that the government of our cities is any worse, in proportion to opportunities, than it was fifty years ago. I'll explain what I mean by 'in proportion to opportunities.' A half a century ago, our cities were small and poor. There wasn't many temptations lyin' around for politicians. There was hardly anything to steal, and hardly any opportunities for even honest graft. A city could count its money every night before goin' to bed, and if three cents was missin', all the fire-bells would be rung. What credit was there in bein' honest under them circumstances? It makes me tired to hear of old codgers back in the thirties or forties boastin' that they retired from politics without a dollar except what they earned in their profession or business. If they lived to-day, with all the existin' opportunities, they would be just the same as twentieth century politicians. There ain't any more honest people in the world just now than the convicts in Sing Sing.[10] Not one of them steals anything. Why? Because they can't. See the application?

"Understand, I ain't defendin' politicians of to-day who steal. The politician who steals is worse than a thief. He is a fool. With the grand opportunities all around for the man with a political pull, there's no excuse for stealin' a cent. The point I want to make is that if there is some stealin' in politics, it don't mean that the politicians of 1905 are, as a class, worse than them of 1835. It just means that the old-timers had nothin' to steal, while the politicians now are surrounded by all kinds of temptations and some of them naturally—the fool ones—buck up against the penal code."

INGRATITUDE IN POLITICS

"There's no crime so mean as ingratitude in politics, but every great statesman from the beginnin' of the world has been up against it. Caesar had his

[10]State prison in Ossining, New York.

Brutus; that king of Shakspere's—Leary, I think you call him—had his own daughters go back on him; Platt had his Odell, and I've got my 'The' McManus. It's a real proof that a man is great when he meets with political ingratitude. Great men have a tender, trustin' nature. So have I—outside of the contractin' and real estate business. In politics I have trusted men who have told me they were my friends, and if traitors have turned up in my camp—well, I only had the same experience as Caesar, Leary, and the others. About my Brutus. McManus, you know, has seven brothers and they call him 'The' because he is the boss of the lot, and to distinguish him from all other McManuses. For several years he was a political bushwhacker. In campaigns he was sometimes on the fence, sometimes on both sides of the fence, and sometimes under the fence. Nobody knew where to find him at any particular time, and nobody trusted him—that is, nobody but me. I thought there was some good in him after all and that, if I took him in hand, I could make a man of him yet.

"I did take him in hand, a few years ago. My friends told me it would be the Brutus-Leary business all over again, but I didn't believe them. I put my trust in 'The.' I nominated him for the Assembly, and he was elected. A year afterwards, when I was runnin' for re-election as Senator, I nominated him for the Assembly again on the ticket with me. What do you think happened? We both carried the Fifteenth Assembly District, but he ran away ahead of me. Just think! Ahead of me in my own district! I was just dazed. When I began to recover, my election district captains came to me and said that McManus had sold me out with the idea of knockin' me out of the Senatorship, and then tryin' to capture the leadership of the district. I couldn't believe it. My trustin' nature couldn't imagine such treachery.

"I sent for McManus and said, with my voice tremblin' with emotions: 'They say you have done me dirt, 'The.' It can't be true. Tell me it ain't true.'

" 'The' almost wept as he said he was innocent.

" 'Never have I done you dirt, George,' he declared. 'Wicked traitors have tried to do you. I don't know just who they are yet, but I'm on their trail, and I'll find them or abjure the name of 'The' McManus. I'm goin' out right now to find them.'

"Well, 'The' kept his word as far as goin' out and findin' the traitors was concerned. He found them all right—and put himself at their head. Oh, no! He didn't have to go far to look for them. He's got them gathered in his club-rooms now, and he's doin' his best to take the leadership from the man that made him. So you see that Caesar and Leary and me's in the same boat, only I'll come out on top while Caesar and Leary went under.

"Now let me tell you that the ingrate in politics never flourishes long. I can give you lots of examples. Look at the men who done up Roscoe

Conkling when he resigned from the United States Senate and went to Albany to ask for a re-election! What's become of them? Passed from view like a movin' picture. Who took Conkling's place in the Senate? Twenty dollars even that you can't remember his name without looking in the almanac. And poor old Platt! He's down and out now and Odell is in the saddle, but that don't mean that he'll always be in the saddle. His enemies are workin' hard all the time to do him, and I wouldn't be a bit surprised if he went out before the next State campaign.

"The politicians who make a lastin' success in politics are the men who are always loyal to their friends—even up to the gate of State prison, if necessary; men who keep their promises and never lie. Richard Croker used to say that tellin' the truth and stickin' to his friends was the political leader's stock in trade. Nobody ever said anything truer, and nobody lived up to it better than Croker. That is why he remained leader of Tammany Hall as long as he wanted to. Every man in the organization trusted him. Sometimes he made mistakes that hurt in campaigns, but they were always on the side of servin' his friends.

"It's the same with Charles F. Murphy. He has always stood by his friends even when it looked like he would be downed for doin' so. Remember how he stuck to McClellan in 1903 when all the Brooklyn leaders were against him, and it seemed as if Tammany was in for a grand smash-up! It's men like Croker and Murphy that stay leaders as long as they live; not men like Brutus and McManus.

"Now I want to tell you why political traitors, in New York City especially, are punished quick. It's because the Irish are in a majority. The Irish, above all people in the world, hates a traitor. You can't hold them back when a traitor of any kind is in sight and, rememberin' old Ireland, they take particular delight in doin' up a political traitor. Most of the voters in my district are Irish or of Irish descent; they've spotted 'The' McManus, and when they get a chance at him at the polls next time, they won't do a thing to him.

"The question has been asked: is a politician ever justified in goin' back on his district leader? I answer: 'No; as long as the leader hustles around and gets all the jobs possible for his constituents.' When the voters elect a man leader, they make a sort of a contract with him. They say, although it ain't written out: 'We've put you here to look out for our interests. You want to see that this district gets all the jobs that's comin' to it. Be faithful to us, and we'll be faithful to you.'

"The district leader promises and that makes a solemn contract. If he lives up to it; spends most of his time chasin' after places in the departments, picks up jobs from railroads and contractors for his followers, and shows himself in all ways a true statesman, then his followers are bound in honor to uphold him, just as they're bound to uphold the Constitution of the United States. But if he only looks after his own interests or shows no talent for scenting out jobs or ain't got the nerve to demand and get his share of the good things that are goin', his followers may be absolved from their allegiance and they may up and swat him without bein' put down as political ingrates."

RECIPROCITY IN PATRONAGE

"Whenever Tammany is whipped at the polls, the people set to predictin' that the organization is goin' to smash. They say we can't get along without the offices and that the district leaders are goin' to desert wholesale. That was what was said after the throw-downs in 1894 and 1901. But it didn't happen, did it? Not one big Tammany man deserted, and to-day the organization is stronger than ever.

"How was that? It was because Tammany has more than one string to its bow.

"I acknowledge that you can't keep an organization together without patronage. Men ain't in politics for nothin'. They want to get somethin' out of it.

"But there is more than one kind of patronage. We lost the public kind, or a greater part of it in 1901, but Tammany has an immense private patronage that keeps things goin' when it gets a set back at the polls.

"Take me, for instance. When Low came in, some of my men lost public jobs, but I fixed them all right. I don't know how many jobs I got for them on the surface and elevated railroads—several hundred.

"I placed a lot more on public works done by contractors, and no Tammany man goes hungry in my district. Plunkitt's O. K. on an application for a job is never turned down, for they all know that Plunkitt and Tammany don't stay out long. See!

"Let me tell you, too, that I got jobs from Republicans in office—Federal and otherwise. When Tammany's on top I do good turns for the Republicans. When they're on top they don't forget me.

"Me and the Republicans are enemies just one day in the year—election day. Then we fight tooth and nail. The rest of the time it's live and let live with us.

"On election day I try to pile up as big a majority as I can against George Wanmaker, the Republican leader of the Fifteenth. Any other day George and I are the best of friends. I can go to him and say: 'George, I want you to place this friend of mine.' He says: 'All right, Senator.' Or vice versa.

"You see, we differ on tariffs and currencies and all them things, but we agree on the main proposition that when a man works in politics, he should get something out of it.

"The politicians have got to stand together this way or there wouldn't be any political parties in a short time. Civil service would gobble up everything, politicians would be on the bum, the republic would fall and soon there would be the cry of: 'Vevey le roi!'

"The very thought of this civil service monster makes my blood boil. I have said a lot about it already, but another instance of its awful work just occurs to me.

"Let me tell you a sad but true story. Last Wednesday a line of carriages wound into Calvary Cemetery. I was in one of them. It was the funeral of a young man from my district—a bright boy that I had great hopes of.

"When he went to school, he was the most patriotic boy in the district. Nobody could sing the 'Star Spangled Banner' like him, nobody was as fond of waving a flag, and nobody shot off as many fire-crackers on the Fourth of July. And when he grew up he made up his mind to serve his country in one of the city departments. There was no way of gettin' there without passin' a civil service examination. Well, he went down to the civil service office and tackled the fool questions. I saw him next day—it was Memorial Day, and soldiers were marchin' and flags flyin' and people cheerin'.

"Where was my young man? Standin' on the corner, scowlin' at the whole show. When I asked him why he was so quiet, he laughed in a wild sort of way and said:

" 'What rot all this is!'

"Just then a band came along playing 'Liberty.'

"He laughed wild again and said: 'Liberty? Rats!'

"I don't guess I need to make a long story of it.

"From the time that young man left the civil service office he lost all patriotism. He didn't care no more for his country. He went to the dogs.

"He ain't the only one. There's a grave-stone over some bright young man's head for every one of them infernal civil service examinations. They are underminin' the manhood of the nation and makin' the Declaration of Independence a farce. We need a new Declaration of Independence—independence of the whole fool civil service business.

"I mention all this now to show why it is that the politicians of two big parties help each other along, and why Tammany men are tolerably happy when not in power in the city. When we win I won't let any deservin' Republican in my neighborhood suffer from hunger or thirst, although, of course, I look out for my own people first.

"Now, I've never gone in for non-partizan business, but I do think that all the leaders of the two parties should get together and make an open, non-partizan fight against civil service, their common enemy. They could keep up their quarrels about imperialism and free silver and high tariff. They don't count for much alongside of civil service, which strikes right at the root of the government.

"The time is fast coming when civil service or the politicians will have to go. And it will be here sooner than they expect if the politicians don't unite, drop all them minor issues for a while and make a stand against the civil service flood that's sweepin' over the country like them floods out West."

BROOKLYNITES NATURAL-BORN HAYSEEDS

"Some people are wonderin' why it is that the Brooklyn Democrats have been sidin' with David B. Hill and the up-State crowd. There's no cause for wonder. I have made a careful study of the Brooklynite, and I can tell you why. It's because a Brooklynite is a natural-born hayseed, and can never become a real New Yorker. He can't be trained into it. Consolidation didn't make him a New Yorker, and nothin' on earth can. A man born in Germany can settle down and become a good New Yorker. So can an Irishman; in fact, the first word an Irish boy learns in the old country is 'New York,' and when he grows up and comes here, he is at home right away. Even a Jap[11] or a Chinaman can become a New Yorker, but a Brooklynite never can.

"And why? Because Brooklyn don't seem to be like any other place on earth. Once let a man grow up amidst Brooklyn's cobblestones, with the odor of Newton Creek and Gowanus Canal ever in his nostrils, and there's no place in the world for him except Brooklyn. And even if he don't grow up there; if he is born there and lives there only in his boyhood and then moves away, he is still beyond redemption. In one of my speeches in the Legislature, I gave an example of this, and it's worth repeatin' now. Soon after I became a leader on the West Side, a quarter of a century ago, I came across a bright boy, about seven years old, who had just been brought over from Brooklyn by his parents. I took an interest in the boy, and when he grew up I brought him

---

[11]Disparaging slang terms like "Japs" for Japanese, "dago" for Italians, and "niggers" for people of color, rightly regarded as unacceptable today, were widely used in Plunkitt's day, and each of these appears in *Plunkitt of Tammany Hall*. Plunkitt believed that the Irish—his ethnic group—were the greatest; he represented a district whose voters were mostly Irish and German, and so he thought little of using derogatory terms to refer to groups other than these. But the assumption of white Anglo-Saxon racial superiority was widespread in American society at the time when the book was published, and many others used derogatory terms to refer to immigrants from southern or eastern Europe or people of color both at home and abroad.

into politics. Finally, I sent him to the Assembly from my district. Now remember that the boy was only seven years old when he left Brooklyn, and was twenty-three when he went to the Assembly. You'd think he had forgotten all about Brooklyn, wouldn't you? I did, but I was dead wrong. When that young fellow got into the Assembly he paid no attention to bills or debates about New York City. He didn't even show any interest in his own district. But just let Brooklyn be mentioned, or a bill be introduced about Gowanus Canal, or the Long Island Railroad, and he was all attention. Nothin' else on earth interested him.

"The end came when I caught him—what do you think I caught him at? One mornin' I went over from the Senate to the Assembly chamber, and there I found my young man readin'—actually readin' a Brooklyn newspaper! When he saw me comin' he tried to hide the paper, but it was too late. I caught him dead to rights, and I said to him: 'Jimmy, I'm afraid New York ain't fascinatin' enough for you. You had better move back to Brooklyn after your present term.' And he did. I met him the other day crossin' the Brooklyn Bridge, carryin' a hobby-horse under one arm, and a doll's carriage under the other, and lookin' perfectly happy.

"McCarren and his men are the same way. They can't get it into their heads that they are New Yorkers, and just tend naturally towards supportin' Hill and his hayseeds against Murphy. I had some hopes of McCarren till lately. He spends so much of his time over here and has seen so much of the world that I thought he might be an exception, and grow out of his Brooklyn surroundings, but his course at Albany shows that there is no exception to the rule. Say, I'd rather take a Hottentot in hand to bring up as a good New Yorker than undertake the job with a Brooklynite. Honest, I would.

"And, by the way, come to think of it, is there really any up-State Democrats left? It has never been proved to my satisfaction that there is any. I know that some up-State members of the State committee call themselves Democrats. Besides these, I know at least six more men above the Bronx who make a livin' out of professin' to be Democrats, and I have just heard of some few more. But if there is any real Democrats up the State, what becomes of them on election day? They certainly don't go near the polls or they vote the Republican ticket. Look at the last three State elections! Roosevelt piled up more than 100,000 majority above the Bronx; Odell piled up about 160,000 majority the first time he ran and 131,000 the second time. About all the Democratic votes cast were polled in New York City. The Republicans can get all the votes they want up the State. Even when we piled up 123,000 majority for Coler in the city in 1902, the Republicans went it 8000 better above the Bronx.

"That's why it makes me mad to hear about up-State Democrats controllin' our State convention, and sayin' who we shall choose for President. It's just like Staten Island undertakin' to dictate to a New York City convention. I remember once a Syracuse man came to Richard Croker at the Democratic Club, handed him a letter of introduction and said: 'I'm lookin' for a job in the Street Cleanin' Department; I'm backed by a hundred up-State Democrats.' Croker looked hard at the man a minute and then said: 'Up-State Democrats! Up-State Democrats! I didn't know there was any up-State Democrats. Just walk up and down a while till I see what an up-State Democrat looks like.'

"Another thing. When a campaign is on, did you ever hear on an up-State Democrat makin' a contribution? Not much. Tammany has had to foot the whole bill, and when any of Hill's men came down to New York to help him in the campaign, we had to pay their board. Whenever money is to be raised, there's nothin' doin' up the State. The Democrats there—always providin' that there is any Democrats there—take to the woods. Supposin' Tammany turned over the campaigns to the Hill men and then held off, what would happen? Why, they would have to hire a shed out in the suburbs of Albany for a headquarters, unless the Democratic National Committee put up for the campaign expenses. Tammany's got the votes and the cash. The Hill crowd's only got hot air."

TAMMANY LEADERS NOT BOOKWORMS

"You hear a lot of talk about the Tammany district leaders bein' illiterate men. If illiterate means havin' common sense, we plead guilty. But if they mean that the Tammany leaders ain't got no education and ain't gents they don't know what they're talkin' about. Of course, we ain't all bookworms and college professors. If we were, Tammany might win an election once in four thousand years. Most of the leaders are plain American citizens, of the people and near to the people, and they have all the education they need to whip the dudes who part their name in the middle and to run the City Government. We've got bookworms, too, in the organization. But we don't make them district leaders. We keep them for ornaments on parade days.

"Tammany Hall is a great big machine, with ever part adjusted delicate to do its own particular work. It runs so smooth that you wouldn't think it was a complicated affair, but it is. Every district leader is fitted to the district he runs and he wouldn't exactly fit any other district. That's the reason Tammany never makes the mistake the Fusion outfit always makes of sendin' men into the districts who don't know the people, and have no sympathy with their peculiarities. We don't put a silk stockin' on the Bowery,[12] nor do we make a man who is handy with his fists leader of the Twenty-ninth. The Fusionists make about the same sort of a mistake that a repeater made at an election in Albany several years ago. He was hired to go to the polls early in a half-dozen election districts and vote on other men's names before these men reached the polls. At one place, when he was asked his name by the poll clerk, he had the nerve to answer 'William Croswell Doane.'

" 'Come off. You ain't Bishop Doane,' said the poll clerk.'

" 'The hell I ain't, you ———' yelled the repeater.

"Now, that is the sort of bad judgment the Fusionists are guilty of. They don't pick men to suit the work they have to do.

"Take me, for instance. My district, the Fifteenth, is made up of all sorts of people, and a cosmopolitan is needed to run it successful. I'm a cosmopolitan. When I get into the silk-stockin' part of the district, I can talk grammar and all that with the best of them. I went to school three winters when I was a boy, and I learned a lot of fancy stuff that I keep for occasions. There ain't a silk stockin' in the district who ain't proud to be seen talkin' with George Washington Plunkitt, and maybe they learn a thing or two from their talks with me. There's one man in the district, a big banker, who said to me one day: 'George, you can sling the most vigorous English I ever heard. You remind me of Senator Hoar of Massachusetts.' Of course, that was puttin' it on too thick; but say, honest, I like Senator Hoar's speeches. He once quoted in the United States Senate some of my remarks on the curse of civil service, and, though he didn't agree with me altogether, I noticed that our ideas are alike in some things, and we both have the knack of puttin' things strong, only he put on more frills to suit his audience.

"As for the common people of the district, I am at home with them at all times. When I go among them, I don't try to show off my grammar, or talk about the Constitution, or how many volts there is in electricity or make it appear in any way that I am better educated than they are. They wouldn't stand for that sort of thing. No; I drop all monkey-shines. So you see, I've got to be several sorts of a man in a single day, a lightnin' change artist, so to speak. But I am one sort of man always in one respect; I stick to my friends high and low, do them a good turn whenever I get a chance, and hunt up all the jobs going for my constituents. There ain't a man in New York who's got such a scent for political jobs as I have. When I get up in the mornin' I can

---

[12]In New York, "the Bowery" referred to the area around Bowery Street, a mile-long boulevard running roughly parallel to Broadway south from Union Square on Manhattan's Lower East Side that was the shopping and entertainment district for a large working-class and immigrant population. "Silk stocking" and "Bowery" were also ways of referring, respectively, to wealthy and poor districts of American cities generally.

almost tell every time whether a job has become vacant over night, and what department it's in and I'm the first man on the ground to get it. Only last week I turned up at the office of Water Register Savage at 9 A.M. and told him I wanted a vacant place in his office for one of my constituents. 'How did you know that O'Brien had got out?' he asked me. 'I smelled it in the air when I got up this mornin',' I answered. Now, that was the fact. I didn't know there was a man in the department named O'Brien, much less that he had got out, but my scent led me to the Water Register's office, and it don't often lead me wrong.

"A cosmopolitan ain't needed in all the other districts, but our men are just the kind to rule. There's Dan Finn, in the Battery district, bluff, jolly Dan, who is now on the bench. Maybe you'd think that a court justice is not the man to hold a district like that, but you're mistaken. Most of the voters of the district are the janitors of the big office buildings on lower Broadway and their helpers. These janitors are the most dignified and haughtiest of men. Even I would have trouble in holding them. Nothin' less than a judge on the bench is good enough for them. Dan does the dignity act with the janitors, and when he is with the boys he hangs up the ermine in the closet and becomes a jolly good fellow.

"Big Tom Foley, leader of the Second district, fits in exactly, too. Tom sells whisky, and good whisky, and he is able to take care of himself against a half dozen thugs if he runs up against them on Cherry Hill or in Chatham Square. Pat Ryder and Johnnie Ahearn of the Third and Fourth districts are just the men for the places. Ahearn's constituents are about half Irishmen and half Jews. He is as popular with one race as with the other. He eats corned beef and kosher meat with equal nonchalance, and it's all the same to him whether he takes off his hat in the church or pulls it down over his ears in the synagogue.

"The other downtown leaders, Barney Martin of the Fifth, Tim Sullivan of the Sixth, Pat Keahon of the Seventh, Florrie Sullivan of the Eighth, Frank Goodwin of the Ninth, Julius Harburger of the Tenth, Pete Dooling of the Eleventh, Joe Scully of the Twelfth, Johnnie Oakley of the Fourteenth, and Pat Keenan of the Sixteenth are just built to suit the people they have to deal with. They don't go in for literary business much downtown, but these men are all real gents, and that's what the people want—even the poorest tenement dwellers. As you go farther uptown you find rather different kind of district leaders. There's Victor Dowling who was until lately the leader of the Twenty-fourth. He's a lulu. He knows the Latin grammar backward. What's strange, he's a sensible young fellow, too. About once in a century we come across a fellow like that in Tammany politics. James J. Martin, leader of the Twenty-seventh, is also something of a hightoner, and publishes a law paper, while Thomas E. Rush, of the Twenty-ninth, is a lawyer, and Isaac Hopper, of the Thirty-first, is a big contractor. The downtown leaders wouldn't do uptown, and vice versa. So, you see, these fool critics don't know what they're talkin' about when they criticise Tammany Hall, the most perfect political machine on earth."

DANGERS OF THE DRESS-SUIT
IN POLITICS

"Puttin' on style don't pay in politics. The people won't stand for it. If you've got an achin' for style, sit down on it till you have made your pile and landed a Supreme Court Justiceship with a fourteen-year term at $17,500 a year, or some job of that kind. Then you've got about all you can get out of politics, and you can afford to wear a dress-suit all day and sleep in it all night if you have a mind to. But, before you have caught onto your life meal-ticket, be simple. Live like your neighbors even if you have the means to live better. Make the poorest man in your district feel that he is your equal, or even a bit superior to you.

"Above all things, avoid a dress-suit. You have no idea of the harm that dress-suits have done in politics. They are not so fatal to young politicians as civil service reform and drink, but they have scores of victims. I will mention one sad case. After the big Tammany victory in 1897, Richard Croker went down to Lakewood to make up the slate of offices for Mayor Van Wyck to distribute. All the district leaders and many more Tammany men went down there, too, to pick up anything good that was goin'. There was nothin' but dress-suits at dinner at Lakewood, and Croker wouldn't let any Tammany men go to dinner without them. Well, a bright young West Side politician, who held a three thousand dollar job in one of the departments, went to Lakewood to ask Croker for something better. He wore a dress-suit for the first time in his life. It was his undoin'. He got stuck on himself. He thought he looked too beautiful for anything, and when he came home he was a changed man. As soon as he got to his house every evenin' he put on that dress-suit and set around in it until bedtime. That didn't satisfy him long. He wanted others to see how beautiful he was in a dress-suit; so he joined dancin' clubs and began goin' to all the balls that was given in town. Soon he began to neglect his family. Then he took to drinkin', and didn't pay any attention to his political work in the district. The end came in less than a year. He was dismissed from the department and went to the dogs. The other day I met him rigged out almost like a hobo, but he still had a dress-suit vest on. When I asked him what he was doin', he said: "Nothin' at present, but I got a promise of a job enrollin' voters at Citizens' Union headquarters." Yes, a dress-suit had brought him that low!

"I'll tell you another case right in my own Assembly District. A few years ago I had as one of my lieutenants a man named Zeke Thompson. He did fine work for me and I thought he had a bright future. One day he came to me, said he intended to buy an option on a house, and asked me to help him out. I like to see a young man acquirin' property and I had so much confidence in Zeke that I put up for him on the house.

"A month or so afterwards I heard strange rumors. People told me that Zeke was beginnin' to put on style. They said he had a billiard-table in his house and had hired Jap servants. I couldn't believe it. The idea of a Democrat, a follower of George Washington Plunkitt in the Fifteenth Assembly District havin' a billiard-table and Jap servants! One mornin' I called at the house to give Zeke a chance to clear himself. A Jap opened the door for me. I saw the billiard-table. Zeke was guilty! When I got over the shock, I said to Zeke: 'You are caught with the goods on. No excuses will go. The Democrats of this district ain't used to dukes and princes and we wouldn't feel comfortable in your company. You'd overpower us. You had better move up to the Nineteenth or Twenty-seventh District, and hang a silk stocking on your door.' He went up to the Nineteenth, turned Republican, and was lookin' for an Albany job the last I heard of him.

"Now, nobody ever saw me puttin' on any style. I'm the same Plunkitt I was when I entered politics forty years ago. That is why the people of the district have confidence in me. If I went into the stylish business, even I, Plunkitt, might be thrown down in the district. That was shown pretty clearly in the senatorial fight last year. A day before the election, my enemies circulated a report that I had ordered a $10,000 automobile and a $125 dress-suit. I sent out contradictions as fast as I could, but I wasn't able to stamp out the infamous slander before the votin' was over, and I suffered some at the polls. The people wouldn't have minded much if I had been accused of robbin' the city treasury, for they're used to slanders of that kind in campaigns, but the automobile and the dress-suit were too much for them.

"Another thing that people won't stand for is showin' off your learnin'. That's just puttin' on style in another way. If you're makin' speeches in a campaign, talk the language the people talk. Don't try to show how the situation is by quotin' Shakspere. Shakspere was all right in his way, but he didn't know anything about Fifteenth District politics. If you know Latin and Greek and have a hankerin' to work them off on somebody, hire a stranger to come to your house and listen to you for a couple of hours; then go out and talk the language of the Fifteenth to the people. I know it's an awful temptation, the hankerin' to show off your learnin'. I've felt it myself, but I always resist it. I know the awful consequences."

ON MUNICIPAL OWNERSHIP

"I am for municipal ownership on one condition—that the civil service law be repealed. It's a grand idea—the city ownin' the railroads, the gas works, and all that. Just see how many thousands of new places there would be for the workers in Tammany! Why, there would be almost enough to go around—if no civil service law stood in the way. My plan is this: first get rid of that infamous law, and then go ahead and by degrees get municipal ownership.

"Some of the reformers are sayin' that municipal ownership won't do because it would give a lot of patronage to the politicians. How those fellows mix things up when they argue! They're givin' the strongest argument in favor of municipal ownership when they say that. Who is better fitted to run the railroads and the gas plants and the ferries than the men who make a business of lookin' after the interests of the city? Who is more anxious to serve the city? Who needs the jobs more?

"Look at the Dock Department! The city owns the docks, and how beautiful Tammany manages them! I can't tell you how many places they provide for our workers. I know there is a lot of talk about dock graft, but that talk comes from the outs. When the Republicans had the docks under Low and Strong, you didn't hear them sayin' anything about graft, did you? No; they just went in and made hay while the sun shone. That's always the case. When the reformers are out they raise the yell that Tammany men should be sent to jail. When they get in, they're so busy keepin' out of jail themselves that they don't have no time to attack Tammany.

"All I want is that municipal ownership be postponed till I get my bill repealin' the civil service law before the next legislature. It would be all a mess if every man who wanted a job would have to run up against a civil service examination. For instance, if a man wanted a job as motorman on a surface car, it's ten to one that they would ask him: 'Who wrote the Latin grammar, and, if so, why did he write it? How many years were you at college? Is there any part of the Greek language you don't know? State all you don't know, and why you don't know it. Give a list of all the sciences with full particulars about each one and how it came to be discovered. Write out word for word the last ten decisions of the United States Supreme Court and show if they conflict with the last ten decisions of the police courts of New York City.'

"Before the would-be motorman left the civil service room, the chances are he would be a raving lunatic. Anyhow I wouldn't like to ride on his car. Just here I want to say one last final word about civil service. In the last ten years I have made an investigation which I've kept quiet till this time. Now I have all the figures together, and I'm ready to announce the result. My investigation was to find out how many civil service reformers, and how many politicians were in state prisons. I discovered that there was forty per cent more civil service reformers among the jail-birds. If any legislative committee wants the detailed figures, I'll prove what I say. I don't want to give the figures now, because I want to keep them to back me up when I go to Albany to get the civil service law repealed. Don't you think that when I've had my inning, the civil service law will go down, and the people will see that the politicians are all right, and that they ought to have the job of runnin' things when municipal ownership comes?

"One thing more about municipal ownership. If the city owned the railroads, etc., salaries would be sure to go up. Higher salaries is the cryin' need of the day. Municipal ownership would increase them all along the line and would stir up such patriotism as New York City never knew before. You can't be patriotic on a salary that just keeps the wolf from the door. Any man who pretends he can will bear watchin'. Keep your hand on your watch and pocket-book when he's about. But, when a man has a good fat salary, he finds himself hummin' 'Hail Columbia,' all unconscious and he fancies, when he's ridin' in a trolley-car, that the wheels are always sayin': 'Yankee Doodle Came to Town.' I know how it is myself. When I got my first good job from the city I bought up all the fire-crackers in my district to salute this glorious country. I couldn't wait for the Fourth of July. I got the boys on the block to fire them off for me, and I felt proud of bein' an American. For a long time after that I use to wake up nights singin' the 'Star Spangled Banner.' "

TAMMANY THE ONLY LASTIN' DEMOCRACY

"I've seen more than one hundred 'Democracies' rise and fall in New York City in the last quarter of a century. At least a half dozen new so-called Democratic organizations are formed every year. All of them go in to down Tammany and take its place, but they seldom last more than a year or two, while Tammany's like the everlastin' rocks, the eternal hills, and the blockades on the 'L' road—it goes on forever.

"I recall off-hand the County Democracy, which was the only real opponent Tammany has had in my time, the Irving Hall Democracy, the New York State Democracy, the German-American Democracy, the Protection Democracy, the Independent County Democracy, the Greater New York

Democracy, the Jimmy O'Brien Democracy, the Delicatessen Dealers' Democracy, the Silver Democracy, and the Italian Democracy. Not one of them is livin' to-day, although I hear somethin' about the ghost of the Greater New York Democracy bein' seen on Broadway once or twice a year.

"In the old days of the County Democracy, a new Democratic organization meant some trouble for Tammany—for a time anyhow. Nowadays a new Democracy means nothin' at all except that about a dozen bone-hunters have got together for one campaign only to try to induce Tammany to give them a job or two, or in order to get in with the reformers for the same purpose. You might think that it would cost a lot of money to get up one of these organizations and keep it goin' for even one campaign, but, Lord bless you! it costs next to nothin'. Jimmy O'Brien brought the manufacture of 'Democracies' down to an exact science, and reduced the cost of production so as to bring it within the reach of all. Any man with $50 can now have a 'Democracy' of his own.

"I've looked into the industry, and can give rock-bottom figures. Here's the items of cost of a new 'Democracy:'

A dinner to twelve bone-hunters	$12.00
A speech on Jeffersonian Democracy	00.00
A proclamation of principles (typewriting) . . .	2.00
Rent of a small room one month for headquarters	12.00
Stationery	2.00
Twelve second-hand chairs	6.00
One second-hand table	2.00
Twenty-nine cuspidors	9.00
Sign-painting	5.00
Total	$50.00

"Is there any reason for wonder then, that 'Democracies' spring up all over when a municipal campaign is comin' on? If you land even one small job, you get a big return on your investment. You don't have to pay for advertisin' in the papers. The New York papers tumble over one another to give columns to any new organization that comes out against Tammany. In describin' the formation of a 'Democracy' on the $50 basis, accordin' to the items I give, the papers would say somethin' like this: 'The organization of the Delicatessen Democracy last night threatens the existence of Tammany Hall. It is a grand move for a new and pure Democracy in this city. Well may the Tammany leaders be alarmed, Panic has already broke loose in Fourteenth Street. The vast crowd that gathered at the launching of the new organization, the stirrin' speeches and the proclamation of principles mean that, at last, there is an uprisin' that will end Tammany's career of corruption. The Delicatessen Democracy will open in a few days spacious headquarters where all true Democrats may gather and prepare for the fight.'

"Say, ain't some of the papers awful gullible about politics? Talk about come-ons from Iowa or Texas—they ain't in it with the childlike simplicity of these papers.

"It's a wonder to me that more men don't go into this kind of manufacturin' industry. It has bigger profits generally than the green-goods business and none of the risks. And you don't have to invest as much as the green-goods men. Just see what good things some of these 'Democracies' got in the last few years! The New York State Democracy in 1897, landed a Supreme Court Justiceship for the man who manufactured the concern—a fourteen-year term at $17,500 a year, that is, $245,000. You see, Tammany was rather scared that year and was bluffed into givin' this job to get the support of the State Democracy which, by the way, went out of business quick and prompt the day after it got this big plum. "The next year the German Democracy landed a place of the same kind. And then see how the Greater New York Democracy worked the game on the reformers in 1901! The men who managed this concern were former Tammanyites who had lost their grip; yet they made the Citizens' Union innocents believe that they were the real thing in the way of reformers, and that they had 100,000 votes back of them. They got the Borough President of Manhattan, the President of the Board of Aldermen, the Register, and a lot of lesser places. It was the greatest bunco game of modern times.

"And then, in 1894, when Strong was elected Mayor, what a harvest it was for all the little 'Democracies' that was made to order that year! Every one of them got somethin' good. In one case, all the nine men in an organization got jobs payin' from $2000 to $5000. I happen to know exactly what it cost to manufacture that organization. It was $42.04. They left out the stationery, and had only twenty-three cuspidors. The extra four cents was for two postage stamps.

"The only reason I can imagine why more men don't go into this industry is because they don't know about it. And just here it strikes me that it might not be wise to publish what I've said. Perhaps if it gets to be known what a snap this manufacture of 'Democracies' is, all the green-goods men, the bunco-steerers, and the young Napoleons of finance, will go into it and the public will be humbugged more than it has been. But, after all, what difference would it make? There's always a certain number of suckers and a certain number of men lookin' for a chance to take them in, and the suckers are sure to be took one way or another. It's the everlastin' law of demand and supply."

CONCERNING GAS IN POLITICS

"Since the eighty-cent gas bill was defeated in Albany, everybody's talkin' about senators bein' bribed. Now, I wasn't in the Senate last session, and I don't know the ins and outs of everything that was done, but I can tell you that the legislators are often hauled over the coals when they are all on the level. I've been there and I know. For instance, when I voted in the Senate in 1904, for the Remsen Bill, that the newspapers called the 'Astoria Gas Grab Bill,' they didn't do a thing to me. The papers kept up a howl about all the supporters of the bill bein' bought up by the Consolidated Gas Company, and the Citizens' Union did me the honor to call me the com-mander-in-chief of the 'Black Horse Cavalry.'

"The fact is that I was workin' for my district all this time, and I wasn't bribed by nobody. There's several of these gas-houses in the district, and I wanted to get them over to Astoria for three reasons: First, because they're nuisances; second, because there's no votes in them for me any longer; third, because—well, I had a little private reason which I'll explain further on. I needn't explain how they're nuisances. They're worse than open sewers. Still, I might have stood that if they hadn't degenerated so much in the last few years.

"Ah, gas-houses ain't what they used to be! Not very long ago, each gas-house was good for a couple of hundred votes. All the men employed in them were Irishmen and Germans who lived in the district. Now, it is all different. The men are dagoes who live across in Jersey and take no interest in the district. What's the use of havin' ill-smellin' gas-houses if there's no votes in them?

"Now, as to my private reason. Well, I'm a business man and go in for any business that's profitable and honest. Real estate is one of my specialties. I know the value of every foot of ground in my district, and I calculated long ago that if them gas-houses was removed, surroundin' property would go up 100 per cent. When the Remsen Bill, providin' for the removal of the gas-houses to Queens County came up, I said to myself: 'George, hasn't your chance come?' I answered: 'Sure.' Then I sized up the chances of the bill. I found it was certain to pass the Senate and the Assembly, and I got assur-ances straight from headquarters that Governor Odell would sign it. Next I came down to the city to find out the mayor's position. I got it straight that he would approve the bill, too.

"Can't you guess what I did then? Like any sane man who had my information, I went in and got options on a lot of the property around the gas-houses. Well, the bill went through the Senate and the Assembly all right and the mayor signed it, but Odell backslided at the last minute and the whole game fell through. If it had succeeded, I guess I would have been accused of graftin'. What I want to know is, what do you call it when I got left and lost a pot of money?

"I not only lost money, but I was abused for votin' for the bill. Wasn't that outrageous? They said I was in with the Consolidated Gas Company and all other kinds of rot, when I was really only workin' for my district and tryin' to turn an honest penny on the side. Anyhow I got a little fun out of the business. When the Remsen Bill was up, I was tryin' to put through a bill of my own—the Spuyten Duyvil Bill, which provided for fillin' in some land under water that the New York Central Railroad wanted. Well, the Remsen managers were afraid of bein' beaten and they went around offerin' to make trades with senators and assemblymen who had bills they were anxious to pass. They came to me and offered six votes for my Spuyten Duyvil Bill in exchange for my vote on the Remsen Bill. I took them up in a hurry, and they felt pretty sore afterwards when they heard I was goin' to vote for the Remsen Bill anyhow.

"A word about that Spuyten Duyvil Bill, I was criticized a lot for introducin' it. They said I was workin' in the interest of the New York Central, and was goin' to get the contract for fillin' in. The fact is, that the fillin' in was a good thing for the city, and if it helped the New York Central, too, what of it? That railroad is a great public institution, and I was never an enemy of public institutions. As to the contract, it hasn't come along yet. If it does come, it will find me at home at all proper and reasonable hours, if there is a good profit in sight.

"The papers and some people are always ready to find wrong motives in what us statesmen do. If we bring about some big improvement that benefits the city and it just happens, as a sort of coincidence, that we make a few dollars out of the improvement, they say we are grafters. But we are used to this kind of ingratitude. It falls to the lot of all statesmen, especially Tammany statesmen. All we can do is to bow our heads in silence and wait till time has cleared our memories.

"Just think of mentionin' dishonest graft in connection with the name of George Washington Plunkitt, the man who gave the city its magnificent chain of parks, its Washington Bridge, its Speedway, its Museum of Natural History, its One Hundred and Fifty-fifth Street Viaduct, and its West Side Court-house! I was the father of the bills that provided for all these; yet, because I supported the Remsen and Spuyten Duyvil Bills, some people have questioned my honest motives. If that's the case, how can you expect legislators to fare who are not the fathers of the parks, the Washington Bridge, the Speedway and the Viaduct?

"Now, understand; I ain't defendin' the senators who killed the eighty-cent gas bill. I don't know why they acted as they did; I only want to impress the idea to go slow before you make up your mind that a man, occupyin' the

exalted position that I held for so many years, has done wrong. For all I
know, these senators may have been as honest and high-minded about the
gas bill as I was about the Remsen and Spuyten Duyvil bills."

PLUNKITT'S FONDEST DREAM

"The time is comin' and, though I'm no youngster, I may see it, when New
York City will break away from the State and become a state itself. It's got
to come. The feelin' between this city and the hayseeds that make a livin' by
plunderin' it is every bit as bitter as the feelin' between the North and South
before the war. And, let me tell you, if there ain't a peaceful separation before
long, we may have the horrors of civil war right here in New York State.
Why, I know a lot of men in my district who would like nothin' better to-day
than to go out gunnin' for hayseeds!

"New York City has got a bigger population than most of the States in
the Union. It's got more wealth than any dozen of them. Yet the people here,
as I explained before, are nothin' but slaves of the Albany gang. We have
stood the slavery a long, long time, but the uprisin' is near at hand. It will
be a fight for liberty, just like the American Revolution. We'll get liberty
peacefully if we can; by cruel war if we must.

"Just think how lovely things would be here if we had a Tammany
Governor and legislature meetin', say in the neighborhood of Fifty-ninth
Street, and a Tammany Mayor and Board of Aldermen doin' business in the
City Hall! How sweet and peaceful everything would go on! The people
wouldn't have to bother about nothin'. Tammany would take care of everything for them in its nice quiet way. You wouldn't hear of any conflicts
between the state and city authorities. They would settle everything pleasant and comfortable at Tammany Hall, and every bill introduced in the
Legislature by Tammany would be sure to go through. The Republicans
wouldn't count.

"Imagine how the city would be built up in a short time! At present we
can't make a public improvement of any consequence without goin' to
Albany for permission, and most of the time we get turned down when we
go there. But, with a Tammany Governor and legislature up at Fifty-ninth
Street, how public works would hum here! The mayor and aldermen could
decide on an improvement, telephone the capitol, have a bill put through in
a jiffy and—there you are. We could have a state constitution, too, which
would extend the debt limit so that we could issue a whole lot more bonds.
As things are now, all the money spent for docks, for instance, is charged
against the city in calculatin' the debt limit, although the Dock Department

provides immense revenues. It's the same with some other departments. This humbug would be dropped if Tammany ruled at the Capitol and the City Hall, and the city would have money to burn.

"Another thing—the constitution of the new state wouldn't have a word about civil service, and if any man dared to introduce any kind of a civil service bill in the Legislature, he would be fired out the window. Then we would have government of the people by the people who were elected to govern them. That's the kind of government Lincoln meant. O what a glorious future for the city! Whenever I think of it I feel like goin' out and celebratin', and I'm really almost sorry that I don't drink.

"You may ask what would become of the up-State people if New York City left them in the lurch and went into the State business on its own account. Well, we wouldn't be under no obligation to provide for them; still I would be in favor of helpin' them along for a while until they could learn to work and earn an honest livin', just like the United States Government looks after the Indians. These hayseeds have been so used to livin' off of New York City that they would be helpless after we left them. It wouldn't do to let them starve. We might make some sort of an appropriation for them for a few years, but it would be with the distinct understandin' that they must get busy right away and learn to support themselves. If, after, say five years, they weren't self-supportin', we could withdraw the appropriation and let them shift for themselves. The plan might succeed and it might not. We'd be doin' our duty anyhow.

"Some persons might say: 'But how about it if the hayseed politicians moved down here and went in to get control of the government of the new state?' We could provide against that easy by passin' a law that these politicians couldn't come below the Bronx without a sort of passport limitin' the time of their stay here, and forbiddin' them to monkey with politics here. I don't know just what kind of a bill would be required to fix this, but with a Tammany constitution, governor, legislature, and mayor, there would be no trouble in settlin' a little matter of that sort.

"Say, I don't wish I was a poet, for if I was, I guess I'd be livin' in a garret on no dollars a week instead of runnin' a great contractin' and transportation business which is doin' pretty well, thank you; but, honest, now, the notion takes me sometimes to yell poetry of the red-hot-hail-glorious-land kind when I think of New York City as a state by itself."

TAMMANY'S PATRIOTISM

"Tammany's the most patriotic organization on earth, notwithstandin' the fact that the civil service law is sappin' the foundations of patriotism all over the country. Nobody pays any attention to the Fourth of July any longer except Tammany and the small boy. When the Fourth comes, the reformers, with Revolutionary names parted in the middle, run off to Newport or the Adirondacks to get out of the way of the noise and everything that reminds them of the glorious day. How different it is with Tammany! The very constitution of the Tammany Society requires that we must assemble at the wigwam on the Fourth, regardless of the weather, and listen to the readin' of the Declaration of Independence and patriotic speeches.

"You ought to attend one of these meetin's. They're a liberal education in patriotism. The great hall up-stairs is filled with five thousand people, suffocatin' from heat and smoke. Every man Jack of these five thousand knows that down in the basement there's a hundred cases of champagne and two hundred kegs of beer ready to flow when the signal is given. Yet that crowd stick to their seats without turnin' a hair while, for four solid hours, the Declaration of Independence is read, long-winded orators speak, and the glee club sings itself hoarse.

"Talk about heroism in the battlefield! That comes and passes away in a moment. You ain't got time to be anything but heroic. But just think of five thousand men sittin' in the hottest place on earth for four long hours, with parched lips and gnawin' stomachs, and knowin' all the time that the delights of the oasis in the desert were only two flights down-stairs! Ah, that is the highest kind of patriotism, the patriotism of long sufferin' and endurance. What man wouldn't rather face a cannon for a minute or two than thirst for four hours, with champagne and beer almost under his nose?

"And then see how they applaud and yell when patriotic things are said! As soon as the man on the platform starts off with 'when, in the course of human events,' word goes around that it's the Declaration of Independence, and a mighty roar goes up. The Declaration ain't a very short document and the crowd has heard it on every Fourth but they give it just as fine a send-off as if it was brand new and awful excitin'. Then the 'long talkers' get in their work, that is two or three orators who are good for an hour each. Heat never has any effect on these men. They use every minute of their time. Sometimes human nature gets the better of a man in the audience and he begins to nod, but he always wakes up with a hurrah for the Declaration of Independence.

"The greatest hero of the occasion is the Grand Sachem of the Tammany Society who presides. He and the rest of us Sachems come on the stage wearin' stove-pipe hats, accordin' to the constitution, but we can shed ours right off, while the Grand Sachem is required to wear his hat all through the celebration. Have you any idea what that means? Four hours under a big silk hat in a hall where the heat registers 110 and the smoke 250! And the Grand Sachem is expected to look pleasant all the time and say nice things when introducin' the speakers! Often his hand goes to his hat, unconscious like, then he catches himself up in time and looks around like a man who is in the tenth story of a burnin' building' seekin' a way to escape. I believe that Fourth-of-July-silk hat shortened the life of one of our Grand Sachems, the late Supreme Court Justice Smyth, and I know that one of our Sachems refused the office of Grand Sachem because he couldn't get up sufficient patriotism to perform this four-hour hat act. You see, there's degrees of patriotism just as there's degrees in everything else.

"You don't hear of the Citizens' Union people holdin' Fourth of July celebrations under a five-pound silk hat, or any other way, do you? The Cits take the Fourth like a dog I had when I was a boy. That dog knew as much as some Cits and he acted just like them about the glorious day. Exactly forty-eight hours before each Fourth of July, the dog left our house on a run and hid himself in the Bronx woods. The day after the Fourth he turned up at home as regular as clockwork. He must have known what a dog is up against on the Fourth. Anyhow, he kept out of the way. The name-parted-in-the-middle aristocrats act in just the same way. They don't want to be annoyed with firecrackers and the Declaration of Independence, and when they see the Fourth comin' they hustle off to the woods like my dog.

"Tammany don't only show its patriotism at Fourth of July celebrations. It's always on deck when the country needs its services. After the Spanish-American War broke out, John J. Scannell, the Tammany leader of the Twenty-fifth district, wrote to Governor Black offerin' to raise a Tammany regiment to go to the front. If you want proof, go to Tammany Hall and see the beautiful set of engrossed resolutions about this regiment. It's true that the Governor didn't accept the offer, but it showed Tammany's patriotism. Some enemies of the organization have said that the offer to raise the regiment was made after the Governor let it be known that no more volunteers were wanted, but that's the talk of envious slanderers.

"Now, a word about Tammany's love for the American flag. Did you ever see Tammany Hall decorated for a celebration? It's just a mass of flags. They even take down the window shades and put flags in place of them. There's flags everywhere except on the floors. We don't care for expense where the American flag is concerned, especially after we have won an election. In 1904 we originated the custom of givin' a small flag to each man as he entered Tammany Hall for the Fourth of July celebration. It took like wild-fire. The men waved their flags whenever they cheered and the sight made me feel so patriotic that I forgot all about civil service for a while. And the good work of the flags didn't stop there. The men carried them home and gave them to the children, and the kids got patriotic, too. Of course, it all cost a pretty penny, but what of that? We had won at the polls the precedin' November, had the offices, and could afford to make an extra investment in patriotism."

ON THE USE OF MONEY IN POLITICS

"The civil service gang is always howlin' about candidates and office-holders puttin' up money for campaigns and about corporations chippin' in. They might as well howl about givin' contributions to churches. A political organization has to have money for its business as well as a church, and who has more right to put up than the men who get the good things that are goin'? Take, for instance, a great political concern like Tammany Hall. It does missionary work like a church, it's got big expenses and it's got to be supported by the faithful. If a corporation sends in a check to help the good work of the Tammany Society, why shouldn't we take it like other mission-ary societies? Of course, the day may come when we'll reject the money of the rich as tainted, but it hadn't come when I left Tammany Hall at 11.25 A.M. to-day.

"Not long ago some newspapers had fits because the Assemblyman from my district said he had put up $500 when he was nominated for the Assem-bly last year. Every politician in town laughed at these papers. I don't think there was even a Citizens' Union man who didn't know that candidates of both parties have to chip in for campaign expenses. The sums they pay are accordin' to their salaries and the length of their terms of office, if elected. Even candidates for the Supreme Court have to fall in line. A Supreme Court Judge in New York County gets $17,500 a year, and he's expected, when nominated, to help along the good cause with a year's salary. Why not? He has fourteen years on the bench ahead of him, and ten thousand other lawyers would be willin' to put up twice as much to be in his shoes. Now, I ain't sayin' that we sell nominations. That's a different thing altogether. There's no auction and no regular biddin'. The man is picked out and somehow he gets to understand what's expected of him in the way of a contribution, and he ponies up—all from gratitude to the organization that honored him, see?

"Let me tell you an instance that shows the difference between sellin' nominations and arrangin' them in the way I described. A few years ago a Republican district leader controlled the nomination for Congress in his Congressional district. Four men wanted it. At first the leader asked for bids privately, but decided at last that the best thing to do was to get the four men together in the back room of a certain saloon and have an open auction. When he had his men lined up, he got on a chair, told about the value of the goods for sale, and asked for bids in regular auctioneer style. The highest bidder got the nomination for $5000. Now, that wasn't right at all. These things ought to be always fixed up nice and quiet.

"As to office-holders, they would be ingrates if they didn't contribute to the organization that put them in office. They needn't be assessed. That would be against the law. But they know what's expected of them, and if they happen to forget they can be reminded polite and courteous. Dan Donegan, who used to be the Wiskinkie of the Tammany Society, and received contributions from grateful office-holders, had a pleasant way of remindin'. If a man forgot his duty to the organization that made him, Dan would call on the man, smile as sweet as you please and say: 'You haven't been round at the Hall lately, have you?' If the man tried to slide around the question, Dan would say: 'It's gettin' awful cold.' Then he would have a fit of shiverin' and walk away. What could be more polite and, at the same time, more to the point? No force, no threats—only a little shiverin' which any man is liable to even in summer.

"Just here, I want to charge one more crime to the infamous civil service law. It has made men turn ungrateful. A dozen years ago, when there wasn't much civil service business in the city government, and when the administration could turn out almost any man holdin' office, Dan's shiver took effect every time and there was no ingratitude in the city departments. But when the civil service law came in and all the clerks got lead-pipe cinches on their jobs, ingratitude spread right away. Dan shivered and shook till his bones rattled, but many of the city employees only laughed at him. One day, I remember, he tackled a clerk in the Public Works Department, who used to give up pretty regular, and, after the usual question, began to shiver. The clerk smiled. Dan shook till his hat fell off. The clerk took ten cents out of his pocket, handed it to Dan and said: 'Poor man! Go and get a drink to warm yourself up.' Wasn't that shameful? And yet, if it hadn't been for the civil service law, that clerk would be contributin' right along to this day.

"The civil service law don't cover everything, however. There's lots of good jobs outside its clutch, and the men that get them are grateful every time. I'm not speakin' of Tammany Hall alone, remember! It's the same with the Republican Federal and State office-holders, and every organization that has or has had jobs to give out—except, of course, the Citizens' Union. The Cits held office only a couple of years and, knowin' that they would never be in again, each Cit office-holder held on for dear life to every dollar that came his way.

"Some people say they can't understand what becomes of all the money that's collected for campaigns. They would understand fast enough if they were district leaders. There's never been half enough money to go around.

Besides the expenses for meetin's, bands, and all that, there's the bigger bill for the district workers who get men to the polls. These workers are mostly men who want to serve their country but can't get jobs in the city departments on account of the civil service law. They do the next best thing by keepin' track of the voters and seein' that they come to the polls and vote the right way. Some of these deservin' citizens have to make enough on registration and election days to keep them the rest of the year. Isn't it right that they should get a share of the campaign money?

"Just remember that there's thirty-five Assembly districts in New York County, and thirty-six district leaders reachin' out for the Tammany dough-bag for somethin' to keep up the patriotism of ten thousand workers, and you wouldn't wonder that the cry for more, more, is goin' up from every district organization now and forevermore. Amen."

THE SUCCESSFUL POLITICIAN
DOES NOT DRINK

"I have explained how to succeed in politics. I want to add that no matter how well you learn to play the political game, you won't make a lastin' success of it if you're a drinkin' man. I never take a drop of any kind of intoxicatin' liquor. I ain't no fanatic. Some of the saloon-keepers are my best friends, and I don't mind goin' into a saloon any day with my friends. But as a matter of business I leave whisky and beer and the rest of that stuff alone. As a matter of business, too, I take for my lieutenants in my district men who don't drink. I tried the other kind for several years, but it didn't pay. They cost too much. For instance, I had a young man who was one of the best hustlers in town. He knew every man in the district, was popular everywhere and could induce a half-dead man to come to the polls on election day. But, regularly, two weeks before election, he started on a drunk, and I had to hire two men to guard him day and night and keep him sober enough to do his work. That cost a lot of money, and I dropped the young man after a while.

"Maybe you think I'm unpopular with the saloon-keepers because I don't drink. You're wrong. The most successful saloon-keepers don't drink themselves and they understand that my temperance is a business proposition, just like their own. I have a saloon under my headquarters. If a saloon-keeper gets into trouble, he always knows that Senator Plunkitt is the man to help him out. If there is a bill in the Legislature makin' it easier for the liquor dealers, I am for it every time. Im a one of the best friends the saloon men have—but I don't drink their whisky. I won't go through the temperance lecture dodge and tell you how many bright young men I've seen fall victims to intemperance; but I'll tell you that I could name dozens—young men who had started on the road to statesmanship, who could carry their districts every time, and who could turn out any vote you wanted at the primaries. I honestly believe that drink is the greatest curse of the day, except, of course, civil service, and that it has driven more young men to ruin than anything except civil service examinations.

"Look at the great leaders of Tammany Hall! No regular drinkers among them. Richard Croker's strongest drink was vichy.[13] Charlie Murphy takes a glass of wine at dinner sometimes, but he don't go beyond that. A drinkin' man wouldn't last two weeks as leader of Tammany Hall. Nor can a man manage an assembly district long if he drinks. He's got to have a clear head all the time. I could name ten men who, in the last few years, lost their grip in their districts because they began drinkin'. There's now thirty-six district leaders in Tammany Hall, and I don't believe a half-dozen of them ever drink anything except at meals. People have got an idea that because the liquor men are with us in campaigns, our district leaders spend most of their time leanin' against bars. There couldn't be a wronger idea. The district leader makes a business of politics, gets his livin' out of it, and, in order to succeed, he's got to keep sober just like in any other business.

"Just take as examples, 'Big Tim' and 'Little Tim' Sullivan. They're known all over the country as the Bowery leaders and, as there's nothin' but saloons on the Bowery, people might think that they are hard drinkers. The fact is that neither of them has ever touched a drop of liquor in his life or even smoked a cigar. Still they don't make no pretences of bein' better than anybody else, and don't go around deliverin' temperance lectures. Big Tim made money out of liquor—sellin' it to other people. That's the only way to get good out of liquor.

"Look at all the Tammany heads of city departments! There's not a real drinkin' man in the lot. Oh, yes, there are some prominent men in the organization who drink sometimes, but they are not the men who have power. They're ornaments, fancy speakers and all that, who make a fine show behind the footlights, but ain't in it when it comes to directin' the city government and the Tammany organization. The men who sit in the executive committee-room at Tammany Hall and direct things are men who celebrate on apollinaris[14] or vichy. Let me tell you what I saw on election night in 1897, when the Tammany ticket swept the city: Up to 10 P.M. Croker,

[13]Bottled water.
[14]Bottled water.

John F. Carroll, Tim Sullivan, Charlie Murphy, and myself sat in the committee-room receivin' returns. When nearly all the city was heard from and we saw that Van Wyck was elected by a big majority, I invited the crowd to go across the street for a little celebration. A lot of small politicians followed us, expectin' to see magnums of champagne opened. The waiters in the restaurant expected it, too, and you never saw a more disgusted lot of waiters when they got our orders. Here's the orders: Croker, vichy and bicarbonate of soda; Carroll, seltzer lemonade; Sullivan, apollinaris; Murphy, vichy; Plunkitt, ditto. Before midnight we were all in bed, and next mornin' we were up bright and early attendin' to business, while other men were nursin' swelled heads. Is there anything the matter with temperance as a pure business proposition?"

BOSSES PRESERVE THE NATION

"When I retired from the Senate, I thought I would take a good, long rest, such a rest as a man needs who has held office for about forty years, and has held four different offices in one year and drawn salaries from three of them at the same time. Drawin' so many salaries is rather fatiguin', you know, and, as I said, I started out for a rest; but when I seen how things were goin' in New York State, and how a great big black shadow hung over us, I said to myself: 'No rest for you, George. Your work ain't done. Your country still needs you and you mustn't lay down yet.'

"What was the great big black shadow? It was the primary election law, amended so as to knock out what are called the party bosses by lettin' in everybody at the primaries and givin' control over them to state officials. Oh, yes, that is a good way to do up the so-called bosses, but, have you ever thought what would become of the country if the bosses were put out of business, and their places were taken by a lot of cart-tail orators and college graduates? It would mean chaos. It would be just like takin' a lot of dry-goods clerks and settin' them to run express trains on the New York Central Railroad. It makes my heart bleed to think of it. Ignorant people are always talkin' against party bosses, but just wait till the bosses are gone! Then, and not until then, will they get the right sort of epitaphs, as Patrick Henry or Robert Emmet said.

"Look at the bosses of Tammany Hall in the last twenty years. What magnificent men! To them New York City owes pretty much all it is to-day. John Kelly, Richard Croker, and Charles F. Murphy—what names in American history compares with them, except Washington and Lincoln? They built up the grand Tammany organization, and the organization built up

New York. Suppose the city had to depend for the last twenty years on irresponsible concerns like the Citizens' Union, where would it be now? You can make a pretty good guess if you recall the Strong and Low administrations when there was no boss, and the heads of departments were at odds all the time with each other, and the Mayor was at odds with the lot of them. They spent so much time in arguin' and makin' grand-stand play, that the interests of the city were forgotten. Another administration of that kind would put New York back a quarter of a century.

"Then see how beautiful a Tammany city government runs, with a so-called boss directin' the whole shootin' match! The machinery moves so noiseless that you wouldn't think there was any. If there's any differences of opinion, the Tammany leader settles them quietly, and his orders go every time. How nice it is for the people to feel that they can get up in the mornin' without bein' afraid of seein' in the papers that the Commissioner of Water Supply has sandbagged the Dock Commissioner, and that the Mayor and heads of the departments have been taken to the police court as witnesses! That's no joke. I remember that, under Strong, some commissioners came very near sandbaggin' one another.

"Of course, the newspapers like the reform administration. Why? Because these administrations, with their daily rows, furnish as racy news as prize-fights or divorce cases. Tammany don't care to get in the papers. It goes right along attendin' to business quietly and only wants to be let alone. That's one reason why the papers are against us.

"Some papers complain that the bosses get rich while devotin' their lives to the interests of the city. What of it? If opportunities for turnin' an honest dollar comes their way, why shouldn't they take advantage of them, just as I have done? As I said, in another talk, there is honest graft and dishonest graft. The bosses go in for the former. There is so much of it in this big town that they would be fools to go in for dishonest graft.

"Now, the primary election law threatens to do away with the boss and make the city government a menagerie. That's why I can't take the rest I counted on. I'm goin' to propose a bill for the next session of the legislature repealin' this dangerous law, and leavin' the primaries entirely to the organizations themselves, as they used to be. Then will return the good old times, when our district leaders could have nice comfortable primary elections at some place selected by themselves and let in only men that they approved of as good Democrats. Who is a better judge of the Democracy of a man who offers his vote than the leader of the district? Who is better equipped to keep out undesirable voters?

"The men who put through the primary law are the same crowd that stand for the civil service blight and they have the same objects in view—

the destruction of governments by party, the downfall of the constitution, and hell generally."

CONCERNING EXCISE

"Although I'm not a drinkin' man myself, I mourn with the poor liquor dealers of New York City, who are taxed and oppressed for the benefit of the farmers up the state. The Raines liquor law is infamous. It takes away nearly all the profits of the saloon-keepers, and then turns in a large part of the money to the State treasury to relieve the hayseeds from taxes. Ah, who knows how many honest, hard-workin' saloon-keepers have been driven to untimely graves by this law! I know personally of a half-dozen who committed suicide because they couldn't pay the enormous license fee, and I have heard of many others. Every time there is an increase of the fee, there is an increase in the suicide record of the city. Now, some of these Republican hayseeds are talkin' about makin' the liquor tax $1500, or even $2000 a year. That would mean the suicide of half of the liquor dealers in the city.

"Just see how these poor fellows are oppressed all around! First, liquor is taxed in the hands of the manufacturer by the United States Government; second, the wholesale dealer pays a special tax to the government; third, the retail dealer is specially taxed by the United States Government; fourth, the retail dealer has to pay a big tax to the State government.

"Now, liquor dealing is criminal or it ain't. If it's criminal, the men engaged in it ought to be sent to prison. If it ain't criminal, they ought to be protected and encouraged to make all the profit they honestly can. If it's right to tax a saloon-keeper $1000, it's right to put a heavy tax on dealers in other beverages—in milk, for instance—and make the dairymen pay up. But what a howl would be raised if a bill was introduced in Albany to compel the farmers to help support the State government! What would be said of a law that put a tax of, say $60 on a grocer, $150 on a dry-goods man, and $500 more if he includes the other goods that are kept in a country store?

"If the Raines law gave the money extorted from the saloon-keepers to the city, there might be some excuse for the tax. We would get some benefit from it, but it gives a big part of the tax to local option localities where the people are always shoutin' that liquor-dealin' is immoral. Ought these good people be subjected to the immoral influence of money taken from the saloons— tainted money? Out of respect for the tender consciences of these pious people, the Raines law ought to exempt them from all contamination from the plunder that comes from the saloon traffic. Say, mark that sarcastic. Some people who ain't used to find sarcasm might think I meant it.

"The Raines people make a pretence that the high license fee promotes temperance. It's just the other way around. It makes more intemperance and, what is as bad, it makes a monopoly in dram-shops. Soon the saloons will be in the hands of a vast trust, and any stuff can be sold for whisky or beer. It's gettin' that way already. Some of the poor liquor dealers in my district have been forced to sell wood alcohol for whisky, and many deaths have followed. A half-dozen men died in a couple of days from this kind of whisky which was forced down their throats by the high liquor tax. If they raise the tax higher, wood alcohol will be too costly, and I guess some dealers will have to get down to kerosene oil and add to the Rockefeller millions.

"The way the Raines law divides the different classes of licenses is also an outrage. The sumptuous hotel-saloons, with $10,000 paintin's and bricky-brac and Oriental splendors gets off easier than a shanty on the rocks, by the water's edge in my district where boatmen drink their grog, and the only ornaments is a three-cornered mirror nailed to the wall, and a chromo[15] of the fight between Tom Hyer and Yankee Sullivan. Besides, a premium is put on places that sell liquor not to be drunk on the premises, but to be taken home. Now, I want to declare that from my experience in New York City, I would rather see rum sold in the dram-shops unlicensed, provided the rum is swallowed on the spot, than to encourage, by a low tax, 'bucket-shops' from which the stuff is carried into the tenements at all hours of the day and night and make drunkenness and debauchery among the women and children. A 'bucket-shop' in the tenement district means a cheap, so-called distillery, where raw spirits, poisonous colorin' matter, and water are sold for brandy and whisky at ten cents a quart, and carried away in buckets and pitchers; I have always noticed that there are many undertakers wherever the 'bucket-shop' flourishes, and they have no dull seasons.

"I want it understood that I'm not an advocate of the liquor dealers or of drinkin'. I think every man would be better off if he didn't take any intoxicatin' drink at all, but as men will drink, they ought to have good stuff without impoverishin' themselves by goin' to fancy places and without riskin' death by goin' to poor places. The State should look after their interests as well as the interests of those who drink nothin' stronger than milk.

"Now, as to the liquor dealers themselves. They ain't the criminals that cantin' hypocrites say they are. I know lots of them and I know that, as a rule, they're good honest citizens who conduct their business in a straight, honorable way. At a convention of the liquor dealers a few years ago, a big city official welcomed them on behalf of the city and said: 'Go on elevatin' your standard higher and higher. Go on with your good work. Heaven will

---

[15]Short for *chromolithograph,* a colored picture.

bless you!' That was puttin' it just a little strong, but the sentiment was all right and I guess the speaker went a bit further than he intended in his enthusiasm over meetin' such a fine set of men and, perhaps, dinin' with them."

A PARTING WORD ON THE FUTURE
OF THE DEMOCRATIC PARTY
IN AMERICA

"The Democratic party of the nation ain't dead, though it's been givin' a lifelike imitation of a corpse for several years. It can't die while it's got Tammany for its backbone. The trouble is that the party's been chasin' after theories and stayin' up nights readin' books instead of studyin' human nature and actin' accordin', as I've advised in tellin' how to hold your district. In two Presidential campaigns, the leaders talked themselves red in the face about silver bein' the best money and gold bein' no good, and they tried to prove it out of books. Do you think the people cared for all that guff? No. They heartily indorsed what Richard Croker said at the Hoffman House one day in 1900. 'What's the use of discussin' what's the best kind of money?' said Croker. 'I'm in favor of all kinds of money—the more the better.' See how a real Tammany statesman can settle in twenty-five words a problem that monopolized two campaigns!

"Then imperialism. The Democratic party spent all its breath on that in the last national campaign. Its position was all right, sure, but you can't get people excited about the Philippines. They've got too much at home to interest them; they're too busy makin' a livin' to bother about the niggers in the Pacific. The party's got to drop all them put-you-to-sleep issues and come out in 1908 for somethin' that will wake the people up; somethin' that will make it worth while to work for the party.

"There's just one issue that would set this country on fire. The Democratic party should say in the first plank of its platform: 'We hereby declare, in national convention assembled, that the paramount issue now, always, and forever, is the abolition of the iniquitous and villainous civil service laws which are destroyin' all patriotism, ruinin' the country, and takin' away good jobs from them that earn them. We pledge ourselves, if our ticket is elected, to repeal those laws at once and put every civil service reformer in jail.'

Just imagine the wild enthusiasm of the party, if that plank was adopted, and the rush of Republicans to join us in restorin' our country to what it was before this college professor's nightmare, called civil service reform, got hold of it! Of course, it would be all right to work in the platform some stuff about the tariff and sound money and the Philippines, as no platform seems to be complete without them, but they wouldn't count. The people would read only the first plank and then hanker for election day to come to put the Democratic party in office.

"I see a vision. I see the civil service monster lyin' flat on the ground. I see the Democratic party standin' over it with foot on its neck and wearin' the crown of victory. I see Thomas Jefferson lookin' out from a cloud and sayin': 'Give him another sockdologer;[16] finish him.' And I see millions of men wavin' their hats and singin' 'Glory Hallelujah!' "

STRENUOUS LIFE OF THE
TAMMANY DISTRICT LEADER

Note: This chapter is based on extracts from Plunkitt's Diary and on my daily observation of the work of the district leader.—W. L. R.

The life of the Tammany district leader is strenuous. To his work is due the wonderful recuperative power of the organization.

One year it goes down in defeat and the prediction is made that it will never again raise its head. The district leader, undaunted by defeat, collects his scattered forces, organizes them as only Tammany knows how to organize, and in a little while the organization is as strong as ever.

No other politician in New York or elsewhere is exactly like the Tammany district leader or works as he does. As a rule, he has no business or occupation other than politics. He plays politics every day and night in the year, and his headquarters bears the inscription, "Never closed."

Everybody in the district knows him. Everybody knows where to find him, and nearly everybody goes to him for assistance of one sort or another, especially the poor of the tenements.

He is always obliging. He will go to the police courts to put in a good word for the "drunks and disorderlies" or pay their fines, if a good word is not effective. He will attend christenings, weddings, and funerals. He will feed the hungry and help bury the dead.

A philanthropist? Not at all. He is playing politics all the time.

Brought up in Tammany Hall, he has learned how to reach the hearts of the great mass of voters. He does not bother about reaching their heads. It is his belief that arguments and campaign literature have never gained votes.

[16]Decisive blow.

He seeks direct contact with the people, does them good turns when he can, and relies on their not forgetting him on election day. His heart is always in his work, too, for his subsistence depends on its results.

If he holds his district and Tammany is in power, he is amply rewarded by a good office and the opportunities that go with it. What these opportunities are has been shown by the quick rise to wealth of so many Tammany district leaders. With the examples before him of Richard Croker, once leader of the Twentieth District; John F. Carroll, formerly leader of the Twenty-ninth; Timothy ("Dry Dollar") Sullivan, late leader of the Sixth, and many others, he can always look forward to riches and ease while he is going through the drudgery of his daily routine.

This is a record of a day's work by Plunkitt:

2 A.M.: Aroused from sleep by the ringing of his doorbell; went to the door and found a bartender, who asked him to go to the police station and bail out a saloon-keeper who had been arrested for violating the excise law. Furnished bail and returned to bed at three o'clock.

6 A.M.: Awakened by fire engines passing his house. Hastened to the scene of the fire, according to the custom of the Tammany district leaders, to give assistance to the fire sufferers, if needed. Met several of his election district captains who are always under orders to look out for fires, which are considered great vote-getters. Found several tenants who had been burned out, took them to a hotel, supplied them with clothes, fed them, and arranged temporary quarters for them until they could rent and furnish new apartments.

8:30 A.M.: Went to the police court to look after his constituents. Found six "drunks." Secured the discharge of four by a timely word with the judge, and paid the fines of two.

9 A.M.: Appeared in the Municipal District Court. Directed one of his district captains to act as counsel for a widow against whom dispossess proceedings had been instituted and obtained an extension of time. Paid the rent of a poor family about to be dispossessed and gave them a dollar for food.

11 A.M.: At home again. Found four men waiting for him. One had been discharged by the Metropolitan Railway Company for neglect of duty, and wanted the district leader to fix things. Another wanted a job on the road. The third sought a place on the Subway and the fourth, a plumber, was looking for work with the Consolidated Gas Company. The district leader spent nearly three hours fixing things for the four men, and succeeded in each case.

3 P.M.: Attended the funeral of an Italian as far as the ferry. Hurried back to make his appearance at the funeral of a Hebrew constituent. Went con-

spicuously to the front both in the Catholic church and the synagogue, and later attended the Hebrew confirmation ceremonies in the synagogue.

7 P.M.: Went to district headquarters and presided over a meeting of election district captains. Each captain submitted a list of all the voters in his district, reported on their attitude toward Tammany, suggested who might be won over and how they could be won, told who were in need, and who were in trouble of any kind and the best way to reach them. District leader took notes and gave orders.

8 P.M.: Went to a church fair. Took chances on everything, bought ice-cream for the young girls and the children. Kissed the little ones, flattered their mothers, and took their fathers out for something down at the corner.

9 P.M.: At the club-house again. Spent $10 on tickets for a church excursion and promised a subscription for a new church-bell. Bought tickets for a base-ball game to be played by two nines from his district. Listened to the complaints of a dozen push-cart peddlers who said they were persecuted by the police and assured them he would go to Police Headquarters in the morning and see about it.

10.30 P.M.: Attended a Hebrew wedding reception and dance. Had previously sent a handsome wedding present to the bride.

12 P.M.: In bed.

That is the actual record of one day in the life of Plunkitt. He does some of the same things every day, but his life is not so monotonous as to be wearisome.

Sometimes the work of a district leader is exciting, especially if he happens to have a rival who intends to make a contest for the leadership at the primaries. In that case, he is even more alert, tries to reach the fires before his rival, sends out runners to look for "drunks and disorderlies" at the police stations, and keeps a very close watch on the obituary columns of the newspapers.

A few years ago there was a bitter contest for the Tammany leadership of the Ninth district between John C. Sheehan and Frank J. Goodwin. Both had had long experience in Tammany politics and both understood every move of the game.

Every morning their agents went to their respective headquarters before seven o'clock and read through the death notices in all the morning papers. If they found that anybody in the district had died, they rushed to the homes of their principals with the information and then there was a race to the house of the deceased to offer condolences, and, if the family were poor, something more substantial.

On the day of the funeral there was another contest. Each faction tried to surpass the other in the number and appearance of the carriages it sent to the funeral, and more than once they almost came to blows at the church or in the cemetery.

On one occasion the Goodwinites played a trick on their adversaries which has since been imitated in other districts. A well-known liquor dealer who had a considerable following died, and both Sheehan and Goodwin were eager to become his political heir by making a big showing at the funeral.

Goodwin managed to catch the enemy napping. He went to all the livery stables in the district, hired all the carriages for the day, and gave orders to two hundred of his men to be on hand as mourners.

Sheehan had never had any trouble about getting all the carriages that he wanted, so he let the matter go until the night before the funeral. Then he found that he could not hire a carriage in the district.

He called his district committee together in a hurry and explained the situation to them. He could get all the vehicles he needed in the adjoining district, he said, but if he did that, Goodwin would rouse the voters of the Ninth by declaring that he (Sheehan), had patronized foreign industries.

Finally, it was decided that there was nothing to do but to go over to Sixth Avenue and Broadway for carriages. Sheehan made a fine turnout at the funeral, but the deceased was hardly in his grave before Goodwin raised the cry of "Protection to home industries," and denounced his rival for patronizing livery-stable keepers outside of his district. The cry had its effect in the primary campaign. At all events, Goodwin was elected leader.

A recent contest for the leadership of the the Second district illustrated further the strenuous work of the Tammany district leaders. The contestants were Patrick Divver, who had managed the district for years, and Thomas F. Foley.

Both were particularly anxious to secure the large Italian vote. They not only attended all the Italian christenings and funerals, but also kept a close lookout for the marriages in order to be on hand with wedding presents.

At first, each had his own reporter in the Italian quarter to keep track of the marriages. Later, Foley conceived a better plan. He hired a man to stay all day at the City Hall marriage bureau, where most Italian couples go through the civil ceremony, and telephone to him at his saloon when anything was doing at the bureau.

Foley had a number of presents ready for use and, whenever he received a telephone message from his man, he hastened to the City Hall with a ring or a watch or a piece of silver and handed it to the bride with his congratulations. As a consequence, when Divver got the news and went to the home of the couple with his present, he always found that Foley had been ahead of him. Toward the end of the campaign, Divver also stationed a man at the marriage bureau and then there were daily foot races and fights between the two heelers.

Sometimes the rivals came into conflict at the death-bed. One night a poor Italian peddler died in Roosevelt Street. The news reached Divver and Foley about the same time, and as they knew the family of the man was destitute, each went to an undertaker and brought him to the Roosevelt Street tenement.

The rivals and the undertakers met at the house and an altercation ensued. After much discussion the Divver undertaker was selected. Foley had more carriages at the funeral, however, and he further impressed the Italian voters by paying the widow's rent for a month, and sending her half a ton of coal and a barrel of flour.

The rivals were put on their mettle toward the end of the campaign by the wedding of a daughter of one of the original Cohens of the Baxter Street region. The Hebrew vote in the district is nearly as large as the Italian vote, and Divver and Foley set out to capture the Cohens and their friends.

They stayed up nights thinking what they would give the bride. Neither knew how much the other was prepared to spend on a wedding present, or what form it would take; so spies were employed by both sides to keep watch on the jewelry stores, and the jewelers of the district were bribed by each side to impart the desired information.

At last Foley heard that Divver had purchased a set of silver knives, forks, and spoons. He at once bought a duplicate set and added a silver tea service. When the presents were displayed at the home of the bride, Divver was not in a pleasant mood and he charged his jeweler with treachery. It may be added that Foley won at the primaries.

One of the fixed duties of a Tammany district leader is to give two outings every summer, one for the men of his district, and the other for the women and children and a beefsteak dinner and a ball every winter. The scene of the outings is, usually, one of the groves along the Sound.[17]

The ambition of the district leader on these occasions is to demonstrate that his men have broken all records in the matter of eating and drinking. He gives out the exact number of pounds of beef, poultry, butter, etc., that they have consumed and professes to know how many potatoes and ears of corn have been served.

According to his figures, the average eating record of each man at the outing is about ten pounds of beef, two or three chickens, a pound of butter, a half peck of potatoes, and two dozen ears of corn. The drinking records, as given out, are still more phenomenal. For some reason, not yet explained, the district leader thinks that his popularity will be greatly increased if he

---

[17]The Long Island Sound, a body of water between the southern coast of Connecticut and the northern shore of Long Island, New York.

can show that his followers can eat and drink more than the followers of any other district leader.

The same idea governs the beefsteak dinners in the winter. It matters not what sort of steak is served or how it is cooked; the district leader considers only the question of quantity, and when he excels all others in this particular, he feels, somehow, that he is a bigger man and deserves more patronage than his associates in the Tammany Executive Committee.

As to the balls, they are the events of the winter in the extreme East Side and West Side society. Mamie and Maggie and Jennie prepare for them months in advance, and their young men save up for the occasion just as they save for the summer trips to Coney Island.

The district leader is in his glory at the opening of the ball. He leads the cotillion with the prettiest woman present—his wife, if he has one, permitting—and spends almost the whole night shaking hands with his constituents. The ball costs him a pretty penny, but he has found that the investment pays.

By these means the Tammany district leader reaches out into the homes of his district, keeps watch not only on the men, but also on the women and children; knows their needs, their likes and dislikes, their troubles and their hopes, and places himself in a position to use his knowledge for the benefit of his organization and himself. Is it any wonder that scandals do not permanently disable Tammany and that it speedily recovers from what seems to be crushing defeat?

THE END

PART TWO

Related Materials

George W. Plunkitt

George W. Plunkitt, Tammany leader of the Eighteenth District, has no office at present, but he has some fat city contracts. He declined a renomination as state Senator last year on account of ill-health. He was born in the Seventeenth District, of Irish parents. He began his career as an ardent advocate of total abstinence, but in later years has not posed prominently in that character. He was politically educated in the school of Boss Tweed, having during the Tweed régime been vice-chairman and virtually chairman of the Tammany committee in what was then the Twenty-second Ward, now the Seventeenth Assembly District. He has been chairman in the district since about 1872. He was a member of the Assembly and of the Board of Aldermen, filling several terms in each during the decade from 1870 to 1880. He was also within the same period superintendent of street-cleaning under Inspector Williams at the time that the Police Department was charged with the duty of cleaning the streets, and during his incumbency the city acquired the reputation of having the dirtiest streets in the world. He was legislated out of office in 1881 by the creation of a separate Department of Street-Cleaning, and in 1883 was elected state Senator, and was subsequently reelected for a second term. His conduct in Albany was most unsavory. The Reform Club "Record" for 1887 said of him: "Mr. Plunkitt is a thoroughly bad Senator. He is in politics as a business. He has no hesitation in using his position for his private gain in the way of assisting his contracts or his real-estate speculations. He is mixed up in every job in the Senate and is the uncompromising foe of all reform in the civil service. He openly admitted that he kept his constituents in subjection by introducing bad bills and keeping them hanging over their heads, adding that his constituents could only be controlled by fear. . . . He was most prolific in introducing bills, some very good and others equally bad; but, good, bad, or indifferent, Mr. Plunkitt was sure to make them inure to his own private benefit in some way. He was prominently mixed up in the cable-railroad legislation, the Western Union tax repeal, the attempt to revive the defunct Metropolitan Transit Company, and various other sweet-smelling schemes." After leaving the Senate he received from the Dock Department contracts for making and repairing docks, which contracts afford him his present occupation. He was a butcher in Washington Market for some years prior to 1870, and was then a poor man. From that time until he obtained the dock contracts, about five years ago, it is not known that he had business other than that of a professional

"George W. Plunkitt," in *Tammany Biographies,* 3rd ed. (New York: Evening Post, 1894).

politician and occupant of public offices. He is reputed to be very wealthy—has been estimated to be twice a millionaire. Speaker James H. Husted is reported to have said of him, "You say Georgie is rich? He ought to be; he never missed an opportunity." Plunkitt is known as the greatest "hustler" in Tammany Hall.

Hon. Geo. W. Plunkitt

Tammany Hall is noted for its broad and liberal men. Its leaders have always been selected from the ranks of the people, and men thus selected must naturally be the choice of the majority of the people. In this great Democratic organization, the name of George W. Plunkitt stands as a guarantee of good faith. Mr. Plunkitt has devoted the best portion of his life in the interests of his constituents, and he has accomplished more than any one man in the organization of which he is an honored member. For sixteen years he has guided the Democracy of his district as a district leader, and for this same number of years he has been seen daily at the famous "Plunkitt" headquarters in City Hall, listening to the grievances of his followers and giving words of good advice, and in other ways attending to the needs of the residents in his district.

George W. Plunkitt is a New Yorker by birth and by education. He was born November 17, 1842, in that portion of New York city now occupied as Central Park, at a place then called the "Negro Village." He was educated in the public schools of this city, and at an early age began to shift for himself. As soon as he was old enough he embarked in business for himself, first starting in Washington Market. His business became very large, and he continued there for over twenty years. Hence Geo. W. Plunkitt's name bears reverence in the Washington Market districts. In later years he went into the business of harbor transportation and general contracting.

During all this time Mr. Plunkitt had a natural desire for political fame, and as early as 1866 he was a candidate for the Assembly. Although he made the campaign on his own personality, he polled the big vote of 1,859, without

"Hon. Geo. W. Plunkitt," *The Tammany Times,* September 21, 1895.

an organization at the back of him. Three years later[1] we find Mr. Plunkitt in Tammany's fold, and he was nominated by that body for Assembly and elected by 1,500 majority in a triangular contest. He was re-elected in 1869, and in 1870 he was elected to the Board of Aldermen, and served from 1870 to 1873. He served with distinction, and always championed the cause of the workingmen. He did not return to public office until 1883, when he was elected to the Senate, and re-elected in 1885. During his term of four years he never was defeated on the floor of the Senate, or had a bill vetoed by either Governors Cleveland or Hill; or in former years by Governor Hoffman, and in later years by Governor Flower.

Again, Mr. Plunkitt took a needed rest of several years, but re-entered public life by being elected to the Senate in 1891 by 7,141 plurality over Michael J. Fenton, Republican, and three minor nominees. Since 1893 he has devoted himself entirely to his numerous private enterprises.

Mr. Plunkitt is known as the "West Side Senator." Among the many bills introduced and passed by him are the Eighth avenue grade from 59th street to 140th street, which established the West Side grade. This was due to his efforts while a member of the Assembly twenty-five years ago.

The public parks for the Twenty-third and Twenty-fourth Wards were also procured through his efforts.

He established the Eleventh District Court, and made provisions for building a new Court House for Civil and Police Court in 54th street, between Eighth and Ninth avenues.

Washington Bridge over the Harlem River was built under the provisions of a bill introduced by him, when a representative from the Eleventh Senatorial District.

He is also the author of the bill providing for the viaduct over One Hundred and Fifty-fifth street, from Amsterdam to Seventh avenue.

He is the champion of the bill for an increase in the salaries of police and firemen in 1885, 1886, and 1887.

For the past twelve years Senator Plunkitt has been chairman of the Committee on Naturalization of Tammany Hall, and the chairman of the Committee on Election Officers for the past ten years; he has likewise been a member of the Committee of Finance for five years in the same organization.

Senator Plunkitt is an excellent debater, an argumentative and forcible speaker, carrying with him that earnestness which is almost certain of conviction; he has thorough knowledge of parliamentary rules, and a personal bearing to all with whom he comes in contact calculated to rally strong

---

[1]These dates are not reliable; the dates in the Introduction to this volume are accurate.

support. He is undoubtedly one of the best-posted men in regards to election laws and New York politics; in fact, he is an encyclopedia of New York political happenings within the past quarter of a century. Personally, Senator Plunkitt is one of nature's noblemen; to know him is to honor and respect him, and for these qualifications he numbers his friends by the thousands. He is a member of numerous social and political organizations, and one of the old members of the Tammany Society and a director in a West Side bank.

Last fall his was the only district that elected their two candidates between Castle Garden and the Bronx River.

Senator Plunkitt is the chairman of the Transportation Committee which is to bring the Tammany delegation to the Syracuse Convention.

Pages 109–110: "Lift the Plunkitt Mortgage!" The front and back sides of a pamphlet distributed by Plunkitt's opponent in the 1904 race for state Senate. *Reminiscences of Martin Saxe,* Oral History Collection of Columbia University.

Two Ways to Lift the Plunkitt Mortgage.

REPUBLICAN WAY—Make a cross (×) mark in the circle under the EAGLE in the Republican column.

DEMOCRATIC WAY—Make a cross (×) mark in the circle under the STAR and then make a cross (×) mark in the voting space in front of the name of MARTIN SAXE in the Republican column.

Two Ways to Lift the Plunkitt Mortgage!

"LIFT THE PLUNKITT MORTGAGE!"

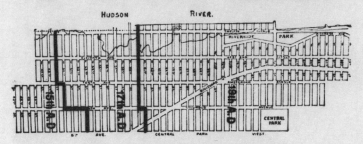

17TH SENATE DISTRICT.

"LIFT THE PLUNKITT MORTGAGE FROM THE 17th SENATE DISTRICT!"

EACH TIME HE MADE A PROMISE! HAS HE KEPT IT?

The People of the 17th Senate District have elected Senator Plunkitt SIX TIMES!

Give Young Men a Chance!

Senator Plunkitt's Promise!

In appealing to the voters of the 17th Senate District for their support in past campaigns, he repeatedly promised, if elected, to remove the New York Central Railroad tracks from Eleventh Avenue. Senator Plunkitt has been elected by the voters of the 17th Senate District SIX TIMES. The railroad tracks are still there and in use!

Abraham Lincoln said: "You can fool ALL the people SOME of the TIME; you can fool SOME of the people ALL of the TIME; but you can't fool ALL the people ALL the TIME!"

Apply Lincoln's words and show Senator "Promising" Plunkitt that the people of the 17th Senate District cannot be fooled ALL the TIME.

"LIFT THE PLUNKITT MORTGAGE FROM THE 17th SENATE DISTRICT!"

HIS OPPONENT

MARTIN SAXE

Regular Republican Nomination
FOR STATE SENATOR
17th Senate District.

' LIFT THE PLUNKITT MORTGAGE FROM THE 17th SENATE DISTRICT!"

Concerning Martin Saxe

He was born a little over thirty years ago in West 50th Street, between Eighth and Ninth Avenues, and has resided all his life in the 17th Senate District. He received his education at Public School No. 69, (in West 54th Street), the Dwight School, Princeton University and the New York Law School. He is a practicing lawyer and a member of the Association of the Bar. From 1902 to 1904 he was the Assistant Corporation Counsel in charge of the Bureau for the Collection of Arrears of Personal Taxes. The work of this bureau is to collect by legal action back personal taxes owing to the city.

From 1898 to 1902 (**FOUR YEARS**) this bureau collected less than **$160,000.** Under Mr. Saxe, from 1902 to 1904 (**TWO YEARS**), this bureau yielded the city over **$600,000.**

Of that amount, **$67,000** was recovered from Senator Plunkitt's friends, the Vanderbilts.

"LIFT THE PLUNKITT MORTGAGE FROM THE 17th SENATE DISTRICT!"

110

Graft, Cries M'Manus; Not Me, Says Plunkitt

A Street Debate on the Cost of Political Favors.

DOCTOR HANDY, NO AUTOPSY

It Ended in Strong Language, and Will Be Renewed in the Fight in the Fifteenth.

George Washington Plunkitt, who used to be a State Senator but is one no longer, and The McManus, whose first name is Thomas, his hated rival for the Tammany leadership of the Fifteenth Assembly District, met on the steps of Police Headquarters yesterday. It was a lively meeting.

When Plunkitt last Fall was defeated by Martin Saxe, a young Republican, for the Senatorship which he had looked upon as a life job, he openly accused The McManus, then his lieutenant, of having sold him out. Since that time Plunkitt and McManus have passed each other without speaking—until yesterday. Meantime on Tuesday evening some anti-Plunkitt history was made in the Fifteenth. The Thomas McManus Association and the Tallahassee Club met then and each nominated a candidate to oppose Plunkitt for the leadership. One of the candidates was The McManus himself, and it is likely that the opposition will unite on him.

Mr. Plunkitt's business at Police Headquarters yesterday was to see Deputy Commissioner McAvoy, but the Deputy Commissioner saw Plunkitt first and found that he had important business somewhere else. By the time he came out Plunkitt's perpetual smile had come off. On the steps he met Senator Frawley and stopped to talk to him. And just then The McManus came along, accompanied by a friend. He in his turn stopped to talk to Coroner's Physician O'Hanlon.

At the sight of McManus Plunkitt said to Senator Frawley, loud enough for McManus to overhear:

"There goes that ingrate. I took that man out of the gutter and made him an Assemblyman."

"Graft, Cries M'Manus; Not Me, Says Plunkitt," *New York Times,* June 8, 1905.

Plunkitt was about to walk away then, but McManus stopped him.

"You took me out of the gutter, did you?" he said; "you're a liar. I paid you $500 for the nomination twice. I paid you that for a job that was worth only $1,500."

"That's a lie," said Plunkitt. "You paid that to the committee."

"Who is the committee?" asked McManus.

"The committee is the committee," retorted Plunkitt.

"And you charged Alderman Richter $500 for a job that paid only $1,000."

"That's another lie," roared Plunkitt. "The committee did it."

"Yes, the committee." McManus laughed scornfully. "Why don't you say your 'little black man' did it?"

Plunkitt was ready to walk away, when McManus took him by the arm and swung him around.

"Perhaps it was 'the committee' or 'the little black man' that went to Albany and did his best to keep me off the Railroad Committee. You know it was you did it."

"You lie again," roared Plunkitt. "Who told you that?"

"Barney Martin told me," McManus answered. "And Speaker Nixon told me the same thing."

Plunkitt turned on his heel and started away. Then he stopped and facing McManus, said:

"Ain't you ashamed of your dirty work trying to destroy an old man like me—a man who has given forty years to the Democratic Party and all his time to the people? I tell you I've got $2,000,000, and I'll spend them and go to the poorhouse or back to the Senate."

"Well, you won't go there," jeered McManus. "McManus may go there himself. I've got you on the hip and I'm going to beat you up there."

Plunkitt departed. O'Hanlon, seeing no further danger of an inquest, went away—in the opposite direction. The McManus, when he found himself in undisputed possession of the field of battle, leaned against the Police Headquarters fence and talked earnestly to Senator Frawley for half an hour. When asked what had brought him to Mulberry Street, he said:

"I came to see Inspector O'Brien of the Detective Bureau regarding a relative of Plunkitt who, at Plunkitt's instigation, has been sending intimidating letters to saloon keepers in the district. Inspector O'Brien was out, but I saw Acting Captain McCauley and he told me I would get the same protection as Plunkitt or anybody else."

Review of
Plunkitt of Tammany Hall

"Plunkitt of Tammany Hall" is the title of a series of plain talks on practical politics delivered by ex-Senator George Washington Plunkitt from his rostrum, the New York County Court House bootblack stand, and recorded by William L. Riordon (McClure, Phillips & Co.). These utterances as reported by Mr. Riordon in several of the New York newspapers have attracted unusual attention, because they have been recognized and accepted at once as the frank self-revelations of a typical Tammany politician. Now that they have attained the dignity of publication in book form, they are likely to be read, not only by New Yorkers, but by Americans everywhere, to whom the mystery of New York politics has a lasting fascination. Especially is there food for reflection in the ex-Senator's chapter on "Honest and Dishonest Graft." One who masters the philosophy of these charming discourses will have mastered the whole secret of New York metropolitan politics—Tammany's secret.

Review of *Plunkitt of Tammany Hall, American Monthly Review of Reviews,* November 1905.

Review of
Plunkitt of Tammany Hall
Tammany Politics

PLUNKITT OF TAMMANY HALL. A Series of Very Plain Talks on Very Practical Politics, Delivered by Ex-Senator George Washington Plunkitt, the Tammany Philosopher, from His Rostrum—the New York County Court-House Bootblack Stand—and Recorded by William L. Riordon. Pp. 183, New York: McClure, Phillips & Co.

Review of *Plunkitt of Tammany Hall, Public Opinion,* October 7, 1905.

"George W. Plunkitt, he seen his opportunities and he took 'em." This is the epitaph of a statesman, written by himself. Mr. Plunkitt's "honest graft" has made him a rich man, even among Tammany men, and his experience has brought to him a very wide and practical bread-and-butter wisdom which he doles out in terse and straightforward English. For more than forty years he has seen the political game played in New York City, and what he doesn't know about it wouldn't be enough to furnish a platform for even a new reform league. His has been the peculiar distinction of holding four offices at one and the same time and drawing salaries for three of them.

Reform and the "civil service" are Mr. Plunkitt's special detestation. His explanation of the ephemeral character of most reform organizations is near enough to the truth to make respectable citizens uncomfortable. He says: "Politics is as much a business as the grocery or the dry goods or the drug business. You've got to be trained up to it or you're sure to fall. Suppose a man who knew nothing about the grocery trade suddenly went into the business and tried to conduct it according to his ideas. Wouldn't he make a mess of it? He might make a splurge for awhile, as long as his money lasted, but the store would soon be empty. It's just the same with a reformer. He hasn't been brought up in the difficult business of politics and he makes a mess of it every time."

But the great danger that is threatening the American people is "civil service." "The time is fast coming when civil service or the politicians will have to go. And it will be here sooner than they expect if the politicians don't unite, drop all them minor issues for awhile and make a stand against the civil service flood that's sweepin' over the country like them floods out west." Plunkitt is an old-fashioned type of the professional politician, even in Tammany Hall, but he has a shrewd, homely sense that is not to be learned from books and that would be invaluable in a man without the moral crookedness that afflicts this man.

Plunkitt Obituary
Plunkitt's Way

George Washington Plunkitt was one of the wisest men in American politics and by a stroke of genius on the part of a good newspaperman, William L. Riordan [*sic*] of the New York *Evening Post,* much of his wisdom was packed into a single small book called "Plunkitt of Tammany Hall." Unfortunately, that book is out of print and rare; but now that Plunkitt is dead it should be republished in large editions and handed to every student of politics, to every organizer of new parties and movements, to every first voter. For in this small book of political sermons, Plunkitt of Tammany Hall, leader of the Fifteenth Assembly District, practical politician and political philosopher, tells all that needs to be told about American government.

He tells why reformers have been only morning glories that "looked lovely in the mornin' and withered up in a short time, while the regular machines went on flourishin' forever like fine old oaks"—a chapter full of post-election thoughts for progressives. He told of the dangers of dress suits and high-priced cars in politics almost twenty years before the defeat of Ramsay MacDonald in England.[1] He explained the difference between honest and dishonest graft in terms so ingenious and yet so simple that Harry Daugherty[2] might have learned a straighter or at least a safer road to wealth and power had he read them; there are no little black bags in the philosophy of George Washington Plunkitt.

He even tells how the Democratic Party can survive. His advice was given in 1905 and in detail may be considered obsolete; but the thought behind it is as good as new and may be applied to 1928 as aptly as to 1908.

> The trouble is [he said] that the party's been chasin' after theories and stayin' up nights readin' books instead of studyin' human nature.... You can't get people excited about the Philippines. They've got too much at home to interest them; they're too busy makin' a livin' to bother about the niggers in the Pacific.... There's just one issue that would set this country

Plunkitt obituary, *The Nation,* December 3, 1924.

[1]Ramsay MacDonald (1866–1937) was the prime minister of the Labor party's first government in England in 1924. He was thought by some to be uncomfortable around his working-class constituents.

[2]Harry Daugherty (1860–1941) was appointed U.S. attorney general by President Warren Harding in 1921. Accused twice of taking bribes, he was dismissed from the post in 1924.

on fire. The Democratic Party should say in the first plank of its platform: "We hereby declare, in national convention assembled, that the paramount issue now, always, and forever is the abolition of the iniquitous and villainous civil-service laws which are destroyin' all patriotism, ruinin' the country, and takin' away good jobs from them that earn them. We pledge ourselves, if our ticket is elected, to repeal those laws at once and put every civil-service reformer in jail." . . .

I see a vision. I see the civil-service monster lyin' flat on the ground. I see the Democratic Party standin' over it with foot on its neck and wearin' the crown of victory. I see Thomas Jefferson lookin' out from a cloud and sayin': "Give him another sockdolager; finish him." And I see millions of men wavin' their hats and singin' "Glory Hallelujah."

Forms change but the fundamental issue remains: enough jobs and enough money to go round. The party that can actually deliver a full dinner pail or the party that promises it convincingly gets the votes. Honesty doesn't matter; efficiency doesn't matter; progressive vision doesn't matter. What matters is the chance of a better job, a better price for wheat, better business conditions. The same issue holds in national elections and in ward politics. General principles, as Mr. Plunkitt says, are all right to work into the platform but they are always going to be side issues.

Reformers who doubt this are bound to be defeated and disillusioned. They must learn somehow to apply the human knowledge that Tammany Hall and George Washington Plunkitt have used for their own ends to the pressing job of salvaging a derelict civilization. They must learn in the first place that politics is a full-time job just like any other business, not a gentlemanly avocation outside of office hours. They must learn that it is a profession requiring training and technique—not merely virtue or indignation. They must learn that it means getting into close, helpful, daily touch with thousands of individuals. "If there's a family in my district in want," said Plunkitt, "I know it before the charitable societies do, and me and my men are first on the ground. The consequences are that the poor look up to George W. Plunkitt as a father, come to him in trouble—and don't forget him on election day." Reformers could learn many a lesson by studying "Plunkitt of Tammany Hall."

Plunkitt worked for himself and for his friends and for his organization. The rest of the people, let us assume, were mulcted[3] by his activities. But they didn't feel it and didn't know it—until he told them. And then they didn't care, because they could understand a cheerful and honest grafter who made no pretense of virtue but did practical good right and left every day

[3]Swindled.

in the week, better than they could a seventh-day reformer who talked of the public welfare and did nothing tangible for anybody.

Plunkitt is dead, but the system he believed in and grew rich by is certainly still a fine old oak. If it is to be hewed down, if the system of private patronage is to be changed to one of honesty and a fair deal all round it will only be by Plunkitt's own method—"You must study human nature and act accordin'."

JANE ADDAMS
Why the Ward Boss Rules

The unusual struggle in Chicago, described in *The Outlook* last week, between the boss of the Nineteenth Ward and Hull House, was, in a measure, precipitated by a paper prepared by Miss Jane Addams, the head of Hull House, for the "International Journal of Ethics," but read at a meeting in Chicago, and so reported by the Chicago daily papers as to stir the wrath of the Alderman described. The entire paper has just appeared in the "International Journal of Ethics," to the courtesy of whose editors The Outlook is indebted for permission to reprint. We have selected those passages which show why the Alderman, who is the most obedient servant of the monopolies, holds a thus far impregnable position in a ward composed of the very poor. The situation presented is so far from confirming the conclusions of pessimists that it awakens new faith in the supremacy of human virtue, when that virtue manifests itself in constant neighborly kindness instead of annual political sermons.

—The Editors

Primitive people, such as the South Italian peasants who live in the Nineteenth Ward, deep down in their hearts admire nothing so much as the good man. The successful candidate must be a good man according to the standards of his constituents. He must not attempt to hold up a morality

Jane Addams, "Why the Ward Boss Rules," *The Outlook,* April 2, 1898.

beyond them, nor must he attempt to reform or change the standard. If he believes what they believe, and does what they are all cherishing a secret ambition to do, he will dazzle them by his success and win their confidence. Any one who has lived among poorer people cannot fail to be impressed with their constant kindness to each other; that unfailing response to the needs and distresses of their neighbors, even when in danger of bankruptcy themselves. This is their reward for living in the midst of poverty. They have constant opportunities for self-sacrifice and generosity, to which, as a rule, they respond. A man stands by his friend when he gets too drunk to take care of himself, when he loses his wife or child, when he is evicted for non-payment of rent, when he is arrested for a petty crime. It seems to such a man entirely fitting that his Alderman should do the same thing on a larger scale—that he should help a constituent out of trouble just because he is in trouble, irrespective of the justice involved.

The Alderman, therefore, bails out his constituents when they are arrested, or says a good word to the police justice when they appear before him for trial; uses his "pull" with the magistrate when they are likely to be fined for a civil misdemeanor, or sees what he can do to "fix up matters" with the State's attorney when the charge is really a serious one.

Because of simple friendliness, the Alderman is expected to pay rent for the hard-pressed tenant when no rent is forthcoming, to find jobs when work is hard to get, to procure and divide among his constituents all the places which he can seize from the City Hall. The Alderman of the Nineteenth Ward at one time made the proud boast that he had two thousand six hundred people in his ward upon the public pay-roll. This, of course, included day-laborers, but each one felt under distinct obligations to him for getting the job.

If we recollect, further, that the franchise-seeking companies pay respectful heed to the applicants backed by the Alderman, the question of voting for the successful man becomes as much an industrial as a political one. An Italian laborer wants a job more than anything else, and quite simply votes for the man who promises him one.

The Alderman may himself be quite sincere in his acts of kindness. In certain stages of moral evolution, a man is incapable of unselfish action the results of which will not benefit some one of his acquaintances; still more, of conduct that does not aim to assist any individual whatsoever; and it is a long step in moral progress to appreciate the work done by the individual for the community.

The Alderman gives presents at weddings and christenings. He seizes these days of family festivities for making friends. It is easiest to reach people in the holiday mood of expansive good will, but on their side it seems natural and kindly that he should do it. The Alderman procures passes from the railroads when his constituents wish to visit friends or to attend the funerals of distant relatives; he buys tickets galore for benefit entertainments given for a widow or a consumptive in peculiar distress; he contributes to prizes which are awarded to the handsomest lady or the most popular man. At a church bazaar, for instance, the Alderman finds the stage all set for his dramatic performance. When others are spending pennies he is spending dollars. Where anxious relatives are canvassing to secure votes for the two most beautiful children who are being voted upon, he recklessly buys votes from both sides, and laughingly declines to say which one he likes the best, buying off the young lady who is persistently determined to find out, with five dollars for the flower bazaar, the posies, of course, to be sent to the sick of the parish. The moral atmosphere of a bazaar suits him exactly. He murmurs many times, "Never mind; the money all goes to the poor," or, "It is all straight enough if the church gets it."

There is something archaic in a community of simple people in their attitude towards death and burial. Nothing so easy to collect money for as a funeral. If the Alderman seizes upon festivities for expressions of his good will, much more does he seize upon periods of sorrow. At a funeral he has the double advantage of ministering to a genuine craving for comfort and solace, and at the same time of assisting at an important social function.

In addition to this, there is among the poor, who have few social occasions, a great desire for a well-arranged funeral, the grade of which almost determines their social standing in the neighborhood. The Alderman saves the very poorest of his constituents from that awful horror of burial by the county; he provides carriages for the poor, who otherwise could not have them; for the more prosperous he sends extra carriages, so that they may invite more friends and have a longer procession; for the most prosperous of all there will be probably only a large "flower-piece." It may be too much to say that all the relatives and friends who ride in the carriages provided by the Alderman's bounty vote for him, but they are certainly influenced by his kindness, and talk of his virtues during the long hours of the ride back and forth from the suburban cemetery. A man who would ask at such a time where all this money comes from would be considered sinister. Many a man at such a time has formulated a lenient judgment of political corruption and has heard kindly speeches which he has remembered on election day. "Ah, well, he has a big Irish heart. He is good to the widow and the fatherless." "He knows the poor better than the big guns who are always about talking civil service and reform."

Indeed, what headway can the notion of civic purity, of honesty of administration, make against this big manifestation of human friendliness, this stalking survival of village kindness? The notions of the civic reformer are negative and impotent before it. The reformers give themselves over largely to criticisms of the present state of affairs, to writing and talking of what the future must be; but their goodness is not dramatic; it is not even concrete and human.

Such an Alderman will keep a standing account with an undertaker, and telephone every week, and sometimes more than once, the kind of outfit he wishes provided for a bereaved constituent, until the sum may roll up into hundreds a year. Such a man understands what the people want, and ministers just as truly to a great human need as the musician or the artist does. I recall an attempt to substitute what we might call a later standard.

A delicate little child was deserted in the Hull House nursery. An investigation showed that it had been born ten days previously in the Cook County Hospital, but no trace could be found of the unfortunate mother. The little thing lived for several weeks, and then, in spite of every care, died. We decided to have it buried by the county, and the wagon was to arrive by eleven o'clock. About nine o'clock in the morning the rumor of this awful deed reached the neighbors. A half-dozen of them came, in a very excited state of mind, to protest. They took up a collection out of their poverty with which to defray a funeral. We were then comparatively new in the neighborhood. We did not realize that we were really shocking a genuine moral sentiment of the community. In our crudeness, we instanced the care and tenderness which had been expended upon the little creature while it was alive; that it had had every attention from a skilled physician and trained nurse; we even intimated that the excited members of the group had not taken part in this, and that it now lay with us to decide that the child should be buried, as it had been born, at the county's expense. It is doubtful whether Hull House has ever done anything which injured it so deeply in the minds of some of its neighbors. We were only forgiven by the most indulgent on the ground that we were spinsters and could not know a mother's heart. No one born and reared in the community could possibly have made a mistake like that. No one who had studied the ethical standards with any care could have bungled so completely.

Last Christmas our Alderman distributed six tons of turkeys, and four or more tons of ducks and geese; but each luckless biped was handed out either by himself or one of his friends with a "Merry Christmas." Inevitably, some families got three or four apiece, but what of that? He had none of the nagging rules of the charitable societies, nor was he ready to declare that, because a man wanted two turkeys for Christmas, he was a scoundrel, who should never be allowed to eat turkey again.

The Alderman's wisdom was again displayed in procuring from downtown friends the sum of three thousand dollars wherewith to uniform and equip a boys' temperance brigade which had been formed in the ward a few months before his campaign. Is it strange that the good leader, whose heart was filled with innocent pride as he looked upon these promising young scions of virtue, should decline to enter into a reform campaign?

The question does, of course, occur to many minds, Where does the money come from with which to dramatize so successfully? The more primitive people accept the truthful statement of its sources without any shock to their moral sense. To their simple minds he gets it "from the rich," and so long as he again gives it out to the poor, as a true Robin Hood, with open hand, they have no objections to offer. Their ethics are quite honestly those of the merry-making foresters. The next less primitive people of the vicinage are quite willing to admit that he leads "the gang" in the City Council, and sells out the city franchises; that he makes deals with the franchise-seeking companies; that he guarantees to steer dubious measures through the Council, for which he demands liberal pay; that he is, in short, a successful boodler.[1] But when there is intellect enough to get this point of view, there is also enough to make the contention that this is universally done; that all the Aldermen do it more or less successfully, but that the Alderman of the Nineteenth Ward is unique in being so generous; that such a state of affairs is to be deplored, of course, but that that is the way business is run, and we are fortunate when a kind-hearted man who is close to the people gets a large share of the boodle; that he serves these franchised companies who employ men in the building and construction of their enterprises, and that they are bound in return to give jobs to his constituency. Even when they are intelligent enough to complete the circle, and to see that the money comes, not from the pockets of the companies' agents, but from the street-car fares of people like themselves, it almost seems as if they would rather pay two cents more each time they ride than give up the consciousness that they have a big, warm-hearted friend at court who will stand by them in an emergency. The sense of just dealing comes apparently much later than the desire for protection and kindness. The Alderman is really elected because he is a good friend and neighbor.

During a campaign a year and a half ago, when a reform league put up a candidate against our corrupt Alderman, and when Hull House worked hard to rally the moral sentiment of the ward in favor of the new man, we encountered another and unexpected difficulty. Finding that it was hard to secure enough local speakers of the moral tone which we desired, we imported orators from other parts of the town, from the "better element," so to speak. Suddenly we heard it rumored on all sides that, while the money and speakers for the reform candidate were coming from the swells, the money which was backing our corrupt Alderman also came from a swell source; it was rumored that the president of a street-car combination, for

---

[1] Recipient of bribes, which were known as "boodle."

whom he performed constant offices in the City Council, was ready to back him to the extent of fifty thousand dollars; that he, too, was a good man, and sat in high places; that he had recently given a large sum of money to an educational institution, and was, therefore, as philanthropic, not to say good and upright, as any man in town; that our Alderman had the sanction of the highest authorities, and that the lecturers who were talking against corruption, and the selling and buying of franchises, were only the cranks, and not the solid business men who had developed and built up Chicago.

All parts of the community are bound together in ethical development. If the so-called more enlightened members of the community accept public gifts from the man who buys up the Council, and the so-called less enlightened members accept individual gifts from the man who sells out the Council, we surely must take our punishment together.

Another curious experience during that campaign was the difference of standards between the imported speakers and the audience. One man, high in the council of the "better element," one evening used as an example of the philanthropic politician an Alderman of the vicinity, recently dead, who was devotedly loved and mourned by his constituents. When the audience caught the familiar name in the midst of the platitudes, they brightened up wonderfully. But, as the speaker went on, they first looked puzzled, then astounded, and gradually their astonishment turned to indignation. The speaker, all unconscious of the situation, went on, imagining, perhaps, that he was addressing his usual audience, and totally unaware that he was perpetrating an outrage upon the finest feelings of the people who were sitting before him. He certainly succeeded in irrevocably injuring the chances of the candidate for whom he was speaking. The speaker's standard of ethics was upright dealing in positions of public trust. The standard of ethics held by his audience was, being good to the poor and speaking gently of the dead. If he considered them corrupt and illiterate voters, they quite honestly held him a blackguard.

If we would hold to our political democracy, some pains must be taken to keep on common ground in our human experiences, and to some solidarity in our ethical conceptions. And if we discover that men of low ideals and corrupt practice are forming popular political standards simply because such men stand by and for and with the people, then nothing remains but to obtain a like sense of identification before we can hope to modify ethical standards.

Hull House, Chicago

LINCOLN STEFFENS

New York: Good Government in Danger

Just about the time this article will appear, Greater New York will be holding
a local election on what has come to be a national question: good government. No doubt there will be other "issues." At this writing (September 15th)
the candidates were not named nor the platforms written, but the regular
politicians hate the main issue, and they have a pretty trick of confusing the
honest mind and splitting the honest vote by raising "local issues" which
would settle themselves under prolonged honest government. So, too, there
will probably be some talk about the effect this election might have upon the
next presidential election; another clever fraud which seldom fails to work
to the advantage of rings and grafters, and to the humiliation and despair
of good citizenship. We have nothing to do with these deceptions. They may
count in New York, they may determine the result, but let them. They are
common moves in the corruptionist's game and, therefore, fair tests of
citizenship, for honesty is not the sole qualification for an honest voter;
intelligence has to play a part, too, and a little intelligence would defeat all
such tricks. Anyhow, they cannot disturb us. I am writing too far ahead, and
my readers, for the most part, will be reading too far away to know or care
anything about them. We can grasp firmly the essential issues involved and
then watch with equanimity the returns for the answer, plain yes or no,
which New York will give to the only questions that concern us all:

Do we Americans really want good government? Do we know it when we
see it? Are we capable of that sustained good citizenship which alone can
make democracy a success? Or, to save our pride, one other: Is the New York
way the right road to permanent reform?

For New York has a good government, or, to be more precise, it has a
good administration. It is not a question there of turning the rascals out and
putting the honest men into their places. The honest men are in, and this
election is to decide whether they are to be kept in, which is a very different
matter. Any people is capable of rising in wrath to overthrow bad rulers.
Philadelphia has done that in its day. New York has done it several times.
With fresh and present outrages to avenge, particular villains to punish, and

Lincoln Steffens, "New York: Good Government in Danger," *McClure's*, November 1903.

the mob sense of common anger to excite, it is an emotional gratification to go out with the crowd and "smash something." This is nothing but revolt, and even monarchies have uprisings to the credit of their subjects. But revolt is not reform, and one revolutionary administration is not good government. That we free Americans are capable of such assertions of our sovereign power, we have proven; our lynchers are demonstrating it every day. That we can go forth singly also, and, without passion, with nothing but mild approval and dull duty to impel us, vote intelligently to sustain a fairly good municipal government, remains to be shown. And that is what New York has the chance to show; New York, the leading exponent of the great American anti-bad government movement for good government.

According to this, the standard course of municipal reform, the politicians are permitted to organize a party on national lines, take over the government, corrupt and deceive the people and run things for the private profit of the boss and his ring, till the corruption becomes rampant and a scandal. Then the reformers combine the opposition: the corrupt and unsatisfied minority, the disgruntled groups of the majority, the reform organizations; they nominate a mixed ticket, headed by a "good business man" for mayor, make a "hot campaign" against the government with "Stop thief" for the cry, and make a "clean sweep." Usually, this effects only the disciplining of the reckless grafters and the improvement of the graft system of corrupt government. The good mayor turns out to be weak or foolish or "not so good." The politicians "come it over him," as they did over the business mayors who followed the "Gas Ring" revolt in Philadelphia, or the people become disgusted as they did with Mayor Strong, who was carried into office by the anti-Tammany rebellion in New York after the Lexow exposures. Philadelphia gave up after its disappointment, and that is what most cities do. The repeated failures of revolutionary reform to accomplish more than the strengthening of the machine has so discredited this method that wide-awake reformers in several cities—Pittsburg, Cincinnati, Cleveland, Detroit, Minneapolis, and others—are following the lead of Chicago.

The Chicago plan does not depend for success upon any one man or any one year's work, nor upon excitement or any sort of bad government. The reformers there have no ward organizations, no machine at all; their appeal is solely to the intelligence of the voter and their power rests upon that. This is democratic and political, not bourgeois and business reform, and it is interesting to note that whereas reformers elsewhere are forever seeking to concentrate all the powers in the mayor, those of Chicago talk of stripping the mayor to a figurehead and giving his powers to the aldermen who directly represent the people, and who change year by year.

The Chicago way is but one way, however, and a new one, and it must be remembered that this plan has not yet produced a good administration. New York has that. Chicago, after seven years' steady work, has a body of aldermen honest enough and competent to defend the city's interests against boodle capital, but that is about all; it has a wretched administration. New York has stuck to the old way. Provincial and self-centered, it hardly knows there is any other. Chicago laughs and other cities wonder, but never mind, New York, by persistence, has at last achieved a good administration. Will the New Yorkers continue it? That is the question. What Chicago has, it has secure. It's [sic] independent citizenship is trained to vote every time and to vote for uninteresting good aldermen. New York has an independent vote of 100,000, a decisive minority, but the voters have been taught to vote only once in a long while, only when excited by picturesque leadership and sensational exposures, only *against*. New York has been so far an anti-bad government, anti-Tammany, not a good government town. Can it vote, without Tammany in to incite it, for a good mayor? I think this election, which will answer this question, should decide other cities how to go about reform.

The administration of Mayor Seth Low may not have been perfect, not in the best European sense: not expert, not coordinated, certainly not wise. Nevertheless, for an American city, it has been not only honest but able, undeniably one of the best in the whole country. Some of the departments have been dishonest; others have been so inefficient that they made the whole administration ridiculous. But what of that? Corruption also is clumsy and makes absurd mistakes when it is new and untrained. The "oaths" and ceremonies and much of the boodling of the St. Louis ring seemed laughable to my corrupt friends in Philadelphia and Tammany Hall, and New York's own Tweed regime was "no joke," only because it was so general, and so expensive—to New York. It took time to perfect the "Philadelphia plan" of misgovernment, and it took time to educate Croker and develop his Tammany Hall. It will take time to evolve masters of the (in America) unstudied art of municipal government—time and demand. So far there has been no market for municipal experts in this country. All we are clamoring for to-day in our meek, weak-hearted way, is that mean, rudimentary virtue miscalled "common honesty." Do we really want it? Certainly Mayor Low is pecuniarily honest. He is more; he is conscientious and experienced and personally efficient. Bred to business, he rose above it, adding to the training he acquired in the conduct of an international commercial house, two terms as Mayor of Brooklyn, and to that again a very effective administration, as president, of the business of Columbia University. He began his mayoralty with a study of the affairs of New York; he has said himself that he devoted eight months to its finances: and he mastered this department and is admitted to be the master in detail of every department which has engaged his attention. In other words, Mr. Low has learned the business of New York; he is just about competent now to become the mayor of a great city. Is there a demand for Mr. Low?

No. When I made my inquiries—before the lying had begun—the Fusion leaders of the anti-Tammany forces, who nominated Mr. Low, said they might renominate him; "who else was there?" they asked. And they thought he "might" be reelected. The alternative was Richard Croker or Charles F. Murphy, his man, for no matter who Tammany's candidate for mayor was, if Tammany won, Tammany's boss would rule. The personal issue was plain enough. Yet was there no assurance for Mr. Low.

Why? There are many forms of the answer given, but they nearly all reduce themselves to one—the man's personality. It is not very engaging. Mr. Low has many respectable qualities, but these never are amiable. "Did you ever see his smile?" said a politician who was trying to account for his instinctive dislike for the Mayor. I had; there is no laughter back of it, no humor, and no sense thereof. The appealing human element is lacking all through. His good abilities are self-sufficient; his dignity is smug; his courtesy seems not kind, his self-reliance is called obstinacy because, though he listens, he seems not to care; though he understands, he shows no sympathy, and when he decides, his reasoning is private. His most useful virtues—probity, intelligence, and conscientiousness—in action are often an irritation; they are so contented. Mr. Low is the bourgeois reformer type. Even where he compromises, he gets no credit; his concessions make the impression of surrenders. A politician can say "no" and make a friend, where Mr. Low will lose one by saying "yes." Cold and impersonal, he cools even his heads of departments. Loyal public service they give, because his taste is for men who would do their duty for their own sake, not for his, and that excellent service the city has had. But members of Mr. Low's administration helped me to characterize him; they could not help it. Mr. Low's is not a lovable character.

But what of that? Why should his colleagues love him? Why should anybody like him? Why should he seek to charm, win affection, and make friends? He was elected to attend to the business of his office and to appoint subordinates who should attend to the business of their offices, not to make "political strength" and win elections. William Travers Jerome, the picturesque District Attorney, whose sincerity and intellectual honesty made sure the election of Mr. Low two years ago, detests him as a bourgeois, but the mayoralty is held in New York to be a bourgeois office. Mr. Low is the ideal product of the New York theory that municipal government is business, not politics, and that a business man who would manage the city as he would a business corporation, would solve for us all our troubles. Chicago reformers think we have got to solve our own problems; that government is political business; that men brought up in politics and experienced in public office will make the best administrators. They have refused to turn from their politician mayor, Carter H. Harrison, for the most ideal business candidate, and I have heard them say that when Chicago was ripe for a better mayor, they would prefer a candidate chosen from among their well-tried aldermen. Again, I say, however, that this is only one way, and New York has another, and this other is the standard American way.

But again I say, also, that the New York way is on trial, for New York has what the whole country has been looking for in all municipal crises—the non-political ruler. Mr. Low's very faults, which I have emphasized for the purpose, emphasize the point. They make it impossible for him to be a politician even if he should wish to be. As for his selfishness, his lack of tact, his coldness—these are of no consequence. He has done his duty all the better for them. Admit that he is uninteresting; what does that matter? He has served the city. Will the city not vote for him because it does not like the way he smiles? Absurd as it sounds, that is what all I have heard against Low amounts to. But to reduce the situation to a further absurdity, let us eliminate altogether the personality of Mr. Low. Let us suppose he has no smile, no courtesy, no dignity, no efficiency, no personality at all; suppose he were an It and had not given New York a good administration, but had only honestly tried. What then?

Tammany Hall? That is the alternative. The Tammany politicians see it just as clear as that, and they are not in the habit of deceiving themselves. They say "it is a Tammany year," "Tammany's turn." They say it and they believe it. They study the people, and they know it is all a matter of citizenship; they admit that they cannot win unless a goodly part of the independent vote goes to them; and still they say they can beat Mr. Low or any other man the anti-Tammany forces may nominate. So we are safe in eliminating Mr. Low and reducing the issue to plain Tammany.

Tammany is bad government; not inefficient, but dishonest; not a party, not a delusion and a snare, hardly known by its party name—Democracy; having little standing in the national councils of the party and caring little for influence outside of the city. Tammany is Tammany, the embodiment of corruption. All the world knows and all the world may know what it is and what it is after. For hypocrisy is not a Tammany vice. Tammany is for Tammany, and the Tammany men say so. Other rings proclaim lies and make pretensions, other rogues talk about the tariff and imperialism. Tammany is honestly dishonest. Time and time again, in private and in public, the leaders, big and little, have said they are out for themselves and their own; not for the public, but for "me and my friends"; not for New York, but for Tammany. Richard Croker said under oath once that he worked for his own pockets all the time, and Tom Grady, the Tammany orator, has brought his crowds to their feet cheering sentiments as primitive, stated with candor as brutal.

The man from Mars would say that such an organization, so self-confessed, could not be very dangerous to an intelligent people. Foreigners marvel at it and at us, and even Americans—Pennsylvanians, for example—cannot understand why we New Yorkers regard Tammany as so formidable. I think I can explain it. Tammany is corruption with consent; it is bad government founded on the suffrages of the people. The Philadelphia machine is more powerful. It rules Philadelphia by fraud and force and does not require the votes of the people. The Philadelphians do not vote for their machines; their machines vote for them. Tammany used to stuff the ballot boxes and intimidate voters; today there is practically none of that. Tammany rules, when it rules, by right of the votes of the people of New York.

Tammany corruption is democratic corruption. That of the Philadelphia ring is rooted in special interests. Tammany, too, is allied with "vested interests"—but Tammany labors under disadvantages not known in Philadelphia. The Philadelphia ring is of the same party that rules the State and the nation, and the local ring forms a living chain with the state and national rings. Tammany is a purely local concern. With a majority only in old New York, it has not only to buy what it wants from the Republican majority in the State, but must trade to get the whole city. Big business everywhere is the chief source of political corruption, and it is one source in New York; but most of the big businesses represented in New York have no plants there. Offices there are, and head offices, of many trusts and railways, for example, but that is all. There are but two railway terminals in the city, and but three railways use them. These have to do more with Albany than New York. So with Wall Street. Philadelphia's stock exchange deals largely in Pennsylvania securities, New York's in those of the whole United States. There is a small Wall Street group that specializes in local corporations, and they are active and give Tammany a Wall Street connection, but the biggest and the majority of our financial leaders, bribers though they may be in other cities and even in New York State, are independent of Tammany Hall and can be honest citizens at home. From this class, indeed, New York can and often does draw some of its reformers. Not so Philadelphia. That bourgeois opposition which has persisted for thirty years in the fight against Tammany corruption, was squelched in Philadelphia after its first great uprising. Matt Quay, through the banks, railways and other business interests, was able to reach it. A large part of his power is negative; there is no opposition. Tammany's power is positive. Tammany cannot reach all the largest interests and its hold is upon the people.

Tammany's democratic corruption rests upon the corruption of the people, the plain people, and there lies its great significance; its grafting system is one in which more individuals share than any I have studied. The people themselves get very little; they come cheap, but they are interested. Divided into districts, the organization subdivides them into precincts or neighborhoods, and their sovereign power, in the form of votes, is bought up by kindness and petty privileges. They are forced to a surrender, when necessary, by intimidation, but the leader and his captains have their hold because they take care of their own. They speak pleasant words, smile friendly smiles, notice the baby, give picnics up the River or the Sound, or a slap on the back; find jobs, most of them at the city's expense, but they have also news-stands, peddling privileges, railroad and other business places to dispense; they permit violations of the law, and, if a man has broken the law without permission, see him through the court. Though a blow in the face is as readily given as a shake of the hand, Tammany kindness is real kindness, and will go far, remember long, and take infinite trouble for a friend.

The power that is gathered up thus cheaply, like garbage, in the districts is concentrated in the district leader who in turn passes it on through a general committee to the boss. This is a form of living government, extralegal, but very actual, and, though the beginnings of it are purely democratic, it develops at each stage into an autocracy. In Philadelphia the boss appoints a district leader and gives him power. Tammany has done that in two or three notable instances, but never without causing a bitter fight which lasts often for years. In Philadelphia the State boss designates the city boss. In New York, Croker has failed signally to maintain vice-bosses whom he appointed. The boss of Tammany Hall is a growth, and just as Croker grew, so has Charles F. Murphy grown up to Croker's place. Again, whereas in Philadelphia the boss and his ring handle and keep almost all of the graft, leaving little to the district leaders, in New York the district leaders share handsomely in the spoils.

There is more to share in New York. It is impossible to estimate the amount of it, not only for me, but for anybody. No Tammany man knows it all. Police friends of mine say that the Tammany leaders never knew how rich police corruption was till the Lexow committee exposed it, and that the politicians who had been content with small presents, contributions, and influence, "did not butt in" for their share till they saw by the testimony of frightened police grafters that the department was worth from four to five millions a year. The items are so incredible that I hesitate to print them. Devery told a friend once that in one year the police graft was "something over $3,000,000." Afterward the syndicate which divided the graft under Devery took in for thirty-six months $400,000 a month from gambling and poolrooms alone. Saloon bribers, disorderly house blackmail, policy, etc., etc., bring this total up to amazing proportions.

Yet this was but one department, and a department that was overlooked by Tammany for years. The annual budget of the city is about $100,000,000, and though the power that comes of the expenditure of that amount is enormous and the opportunities for rake-offs infinite, this sum is not one-half of the resources of Tammany when it is in power. Her resources are the resources of the city as a business, as a political, as a social power. If Tammany could be incorporated and all its earnings, both legitimate and illegitimate, gathered up and paid over in dividends, the stockholders would get more than the New York Central bond and stockholders, more than the Standard Oil stockholders, and the controlling clique would wield a power equal to that of the United States Steel Company. Tammany, when in control of New York, takes out of the city unbelievable millions of dollars a year.

No wonder the leaders are all rich; no wonder so many more Tammany men are rich than are the leaders in any other town; no wonder Tammany is liberal in its division of the graft. Croker took the best and the safest of it, and he accepted shares in others. He was "in on the Wall Street end," and the Tammany clique of financiers have knocked down and bought up at low prices Manhattan Railway stock by threats of the city's power over the road; they have been let in on Metropolitan deals and on the Third Avenue Railroad grab; the Ice Trust is a Tammany trust; they have banks and trust companies, and through the New York Realty Company are forcing alliances with such financial groups as that of the Standard Oil Company. Croker shared in these deals and businesses. He sold judgeships, taking his pay in the form of contributions to the Tammany campaign fund, of which he was treasurer, and he had the judges take from the regular real estate exchange all the enormous real estate business that passed through the courts, and give it to an exchange connected with the real estate business of his firm, Peter F. Meyer & Co. This alone would maintain a ducal estate in England. But his real estate business was greater than that. It had extraordinary legal facilities, the free advertising of abuse, the prestige of political privilege, all of which brought in trade; and it had advance information and followed with profitable deals, great public improvements.

Though Croker said he worked for his own pockets all the time, and did take the best of the graft, he was not "hoggish." One of the richest graft in the city is in the Department of Buildings. $100,000,000 a year goes into building operations in New York. All of this, from out-houses to skyscrapers, is subject to very precise laws and regulations, most of them wise, some impossible. The Building Department has the enforcement of these; it passes upon all construction, private and public, at all stages from plan-making to actual completion; and can cause not only "unavoidable delay" but can wink at most profitable violations. Architects and builders had to stand in with the department. They called on the right man and they settled on a scale which was not fixed, but which generally was on the basis of the department's estimate of a fair half of the value of the saving in time or bad material. This brought in at least a banker's percentage on one hundred millions a year. Croker, so far as I can make out, took none of this; it was let out to other leaders and was their own graft.

District Attorney William Travers Jerome has looked into the Dock Department, and he knows things which he yet may prove. This is an important investigation for two reasons. It is very large graft and the new Tammany leader, Charlie Murphy, had it. New York wants to know more about Murphy, and it should want to know about the management of its docks, since, just as other cities have their corrupt dealings with railways and their terminals, so New York's great terminal business is with steamships and docks. These docks should pay the city handsomely. Mr. Murphy says they shouldn't; he is wise, as Croker was before he became old and garrulous, and, as Tammany men put it, "keeps his mouth shut," but he did say that the docks should not be run for revenue to the city but for their own improvement. The Dock Board has exclusive and private and secret control of the expenditure of $10,000,000 a year. No wonder Murphy chose it.

It is impossible to follow all New York graft from its source to its final destination. It is impossible to follow here the course of that which is well known to New Yorkers. There are public works for Tammany contractors. There are private works for Tammany contractors, and corporations and individuals find it expedient to let it go to Tammany contractors. Tammany has a very good system of grafting on public works; I mean that it is "good" from the criminal point of view—and so it has for the furnishing of supplies. Low bids and short deliveries, generally speaking (and that is the only way I can speak here), is the method. But the Tammany system, as a whole, is weak.

Tammany men as grafters have a confidence in their methods and system, which, in the light of such perfection as that of Philadelphia, is amusing, and the average New Yorker takes in "the organization" a queer sort of pride, which is ignorant and provincial. Tammany is 'way behind the times. It is growing; it has improved. In Tweed's day the politicians stole from the city treasury, divided the money on the steps of the City Hall, and, not only the leaders, big and little, but heelers and outsiders; not only Tweed, but ward carpenters robbed the city; not only politicians, but newspapers and citizens were "in on the divvy." New York, not Tammany alone, was corrupt. When the exposure came, and Tweed asked his famous question, "What are you going to do about it?" the ring mayor, A. Oakey Hall, asked another as significant. It was reported that suit was to be brought against the ring to recover stolen funds. "Who is going to sue?" said Mayor Hall, who could not think of anybody of importance sufficiently without sin to throw the first stone. Stealing was stopped and grafting was made more business-like, but still it was too general, and the boodling for the Broadway street railway franchise prompted a still closer grip on the business. The organization since then has been gradually concentrating the control of graft. Croker did not proceed so far along the line as the Philadelphia ring has, as the police scandals showed. After the Lexow exposures, Tammany took over that graft, but still let it go practically by districts, and the police captains still got a third. After the Mazet exposures, Devery became Chief and the police graft was so concentrated that the division was reduced to fourteen parts. Again, later, it was reduced to a syndicate of four or five men, with a dribble of miscellaneous graft for the police. In Philadelphia the police have nothing to do with the police graft; a policeman may collect it, but he acts for a politician, who in turn passes it up to a small ring. That is the drift in New York. Under Devery the police officers got comparatively little, and the rank and file themselves were blackmailed for transfers and promotions, for remittances of fines, and in a dozen other petty ways.

Philadelphia is the end toward which New York under Tammany is driving as fast as the lower intelligence and higher conceit of its leaders will let it. In Philadelphia one very small ring gets everything, dividing the whole as it pleases, and not all those in the inner ring are politicians. Trusting few individuals, they are safe from exposure, more powerful, more deliberate, and they are wise as politicians. When, as in New York, the number of grafters is large, this delicate business is in some hands that are rapacious. The police grafters, for example, in Devery's day, were not content with the amounts collected from the big vices. They cultivated minor vices, like policy, to such an extent that the Policy King was caught and sent to prison, and Devery's wardman, Glennon, was pushed into so tight a hole that there was danger that District Attorney Jerome would get past Glennon to Devery and the syndicate. The murder of a witness the night he was in the Tenderloin police station served to save the day. But, worst of all, Tammany, the "friend of the people," permitted the organization of a band of so-called Cadets, who made a business, under the protection of the police, of ruining the daughters of the tenements and even of catching and imprisoning in disorderly houses the wives of poor men. This horrid traffic never was exposed; it could not and cannot be. Vicious women were "planted" in tenement houses and (I know this personally) the children of decent parents counted the customers, witnessed their transactions with these creatures, and, as a father told with shame and tears, reported totals at the family table.

Tammany leaders are usually the natural leaders of the people in these districts, and they are originally good-natured, kindly men. No one has a more sincere liking than I for some of those common but generous fellows; their charity is real, at first. But they sell out their own people. They do give them coal and help them in their private troubles, but, as they grow rich and powerful, the kindness goes out of the charity and they not only collect at their saloons or in rents—cash for their "goodness"; they not only ruin fathers and sons and cause the troubles they relieve; they sacrifice the children in the schools; let the Health Department neglect the tenements, and, worst of all, plant vice in neighborhood and in the homes of the poor.

This is not only bad; it is bad politics; it has defeated Tammany. Woe to New York when Tammany learns better. Honest fools talk of the reform of Tammany Hall. It is an old hope, this, and twice it has been disappointed, but it is not vain. That is the real danger ahead. The reform of a corrupt ring means, as I have said before, the reform of its system of grafting and a wise consideration of certain features of good government. Croker turned his "best chief of police," William S. Devery, out of Tammany Hall, and, slow and old as he was, Croker learned what clean streets were from Col. Waring, and gave them. Now there is a new boss, a young man, Charles F. Murphy, and unknown to New Yorkers. He looks dense, but he acts with force, decision, and skill. The new mayor will be his man. He may divide with Croker and leave to the "old man" all his accustomed graft, but Charlie Murphy will rule Tammany and, if Tammany is elected, New York also. Lewis Nixon is urging Murphy publicly, as I write, to declare against the police scandals and all the worst practices of Tammany. Lewis Nixon is an honest man, but he was one of the men Croker tried to appoint leader of Tammany Hall. And when he resigned Mr. Nixon said that he found that a man could could not keep that leadership and his self-respect. Yet Mr. Nixon is a type of the man who thinks Tammany would be fit to rule New York if the organization would "reform."

As a New Yorker, I fear Murphy will prove sagacious enough to do just that: stop the scandals, put all the graft in the hands of a few tried and true men, and give the city what it would call good government. Murphy says he will nominate for mayor a man so "good" that his goodness will astonish New York. I don't fear a bad Tammany mayor; I dread the election of a good one. For I have been to Philadelphia.

Philadelphia had a bad ring mayor, a man who promoted the graft and caused scandal after scandal. The leaders there, the wisest political grafters in this country, learned a great lesson from that. As one of them said to me:

"The American people don't mind grafting, but they hate scandals. They don't kick so much on a jiggered public contract for a boulevard, but they want the boulevard and no fuss and no dust. We want to give them that. We want to give them what they really want, a quiet Sabbath, safe streets, orderly nights, and homes secure. They let us have the police graft. But this mayor was a hog. You see, he had but one term and he could get a share only on what was made in his term. He not only took a hog's share off what was coming, but he wanted everything to come in his term. So I'm down on grafting mayors and grafting office-holders. I tell you it's good politics to have honest men in office. I mean men that are personally honest."

So they got John Weaver for Mayor, and honest John Weaver is checking corruption, restoring order, and doing a great many good things, which it is "good politics" to do. For he is satisfying the people, soothing their ruffled pride, and reconciling them to machine rule. I have letters from friends of mine there, honest men, who wish me to bear witness to the goodness of Mayor Weaver. I do. And I believe that if the Philadelphia machine leaders are as careful with Mayor Weaver as they have been and let him continue to give to the end as good government as he has given so far, the "Philadelphia plan" of graft will last and Philadelphia will never again be a free American city.

Philadelphia and New York began about the same time, some thirty years ago, to reform their city governments. Philadelphia got "good government"—what the Philadelphians call good—from a corrupt ring and quit, satisfied to be a scandal to the nation and a disgrace to democracy. New York has gone on fighting, advancing and retreating, for thirty years till now it has achieved the beginnings, under Mayor Low, of a government for the people. Do the New Yorkers know it? Do they care? They are Americans, mixed and typical; do we Americans really want good government? Or, as I said at starting, have they worked for thirty years along the wrong road—crowded with unhappy American cities—the road to Philadelphia and despair?

A Plunkitt Chronology
(1842–1924)

1842: George Washington Plunkitt born on November 17 in New York City.

1850: Attends public school and lives with parents, Patrick and Sarah, and brothers, David and Dan.

1853–60: Leaves school and works successively as cart driver, apprentice brush maker, and apprentice butcher.

1865: First listed as butcher in New York City Directory, with shop at 17 Washington Market.

1866: Defeated in his first run for office as independent candidate for New York State Assembly.

1868: Elected to Assembly on Tammany ticket.

1869: Reelected to state Assembly.

1870: While still serving in state Assembly, elected to terms on New York Board of Aldermen and Board of Supervisors of county of New York, held until 1873 while at the same time serving as an acting police magistrate for two years and beginning a six-year term as deputy street commissioner.

1876: Sells butcher shop to work in contracting, real estate development, and politics.

1880: Elected Tammany Hall district leader of the middle West Side State Assembly district in which he lives; as such also serves on executive committee of Tammany Hall Democracy. Holds these positions until 1905.

1882: Initiated into Tammany Society or Columbian Order.

1883: Elected on Tammany ticket to New York State Senate; begins serving as chairman of Tammany Democracy's naturalization committee.

1885:   Reelected to state Senate; serves as chairman of Tammany Democracy's Committee on Election Officers.

1887:   Defeated for renomination to state Senate.

1890:   Member of Tammany Democracy's finance committee. Denounced by New York *Evening Post* editor E. L. Godkin in the first edition of the "Tammany Biographies."

1891:   Elected again to state Senate.

1893:   Refuses renomination for state Senate because of poor health.

1895:   Serves as chairman of Tammany Democracy's transportation committee; in charge of arranging transportation of Tammany delegates to state and national conventions of the Democratic party.

1897:   Interviews with reporter William L. Riordon begin appearing in New York *Evening Post*. Elected to one-year term as one of thirteen "sachems" in charge of Tammany Society.

1898:   Elected again to state Senate.

1900:   Reelected to state Senate. Elected sachem of Tammany Society; holds latter position until his death.

1902:   Reelected to state Senate; elected Father of the Council of Sachems of the Tammany Society.

1904:   Defeated for reelection to state Senate by Martin Saxe. Lincoln Steffens's book *The Shame of the Cities* published.

1905:   *Plunkitt of Tammany Hall* published; Plunkitt defeated for reelection to Tammany Democracy district leadership by Thomas J. "The" McManus.

1907:   Defeated in attempt to retake Tammany district leadership from McManus.

1924:   Dies in New York on November 19.

Selected Bibliography

Because they have been important realities in and icons of American politics for more than one hundred years, urban bosses and machines have been the subject of numerous works by journalists, historians, and others. Rather than plunging into this literature directly, it is best to begin with historiographical surveys of the literature that point out the ways that the view of the boss has developed over time. Useful recent surveys include Terrence J. McDonald, "The Burdens of Urban History: The Theory of the State in Recent American Social History," *Studies in American Political Development* 3 (1989): 3–29; Zane Miller, "Bosses, Machines, and the Urban Political Process," in Scott Greer, ed., *Ethnics, Machines, and the American Urban Future* (Cambridge, Mass.: Schenkman, 1981); Bruce M. Stave et al., "A Reassessment of the Urban Political Boss: An Exchange of Views," *The History Teacher* 21 (1988): 293–312; and Jon C. Teaford, *"Finis* for Tweed and Steffens: Rewriting the History of Urban Rule," *Reviews in American History* 10 (1982): 143–53. An older essay on the issues raised in the study of machine politics that still repays reading is Raymond Wolfinger, "Why Political Machines Have Not Withered Away and Other Revisionist Thoughts," *Journal of Politics* 34 (1972): 365–98. Bruce M. Stave has helpfully collected samples of opinion on the political machine from the late nineteenth century to the present in *Urban Bosses, Machines, and Progressive Reformers* (Malabar, Fla.: Robert Krieger Publishing Co., 1984), and that collection also contains a very useful bibliography.

Most recent work on bosses and machines has stressed the limitations on their power by focusing on the structural conditions affecting the rise and demise of machines or emphasizing the role of other actors on the urban political scene. After a careful study of accounts of machine politics in the nation's largest cities, M. Craig Brown and Charles N. Halaby have argued that there were fewer powerful citywide machines than might have been expected, in "Machine Politics in America, 1870–1945," *Journal of Interdisciplinary History* 17 (1987): 587–

612. Alan DiGaetano has focused on the structural conditions undergirding the rise and fall of machines in "The Rise and Development of Urban Political Machines," *Urban Affairs Quarterly* 24 (1988): 242–67, and Harvey Boulay and Alan DiGaetano, "Why Did Political Machines Disappear?," *Journal of Urban History* 12 (1985): 25–49. In *The Unheralded Triumph: City Government in America, 1870–1900* (Baltimore: Johns Hopkins University Press, 1984), Jon C. Teaford argues that other actors were more important than bosses in the overall development of urban government, and Terrence J. McDonald makes a similar point in a single-city case study, *The Parameters of Urban Fiscal Policy: Socioeconomic Change and Political Culture in San Francisco, 1860–1906* (Berkeley: University of California Press, 1986). Steven Erie offers a very thoughtful overview of machine politics from this perspective in *Rainbow's End: Irish Americans and the Dilemmas of Urban Machine Politics, 1840–1985* (Berkeley: University of California Press, 1988). Erie's book also contains an extensive bibliography of works by political scientists and historians on political machines. These newer views have been applied to Tammany Hall itself in Martin Shefter's essays, "The Emergence of the Political Machine: An Alternative View," in Willis Hawley et al., *Theoretical Perspectives on Urban Politics* (Englewood Cliffs, N.J.: Prentice Hall, 1976), and "The Electoral Foundations of the Political Machine: New York City, 1884–1897," in Joel H. Silbey, Allan A. Bogue, and William H. Flanigan, eds., *The History of American Electoral Behavior* (Princeton: Princeton University Press, 1978), and in recent books including Amy Bridges, *A City in the Republic: Antebellum New York and the Origins of Machine Politics* (Cambridge, Eng.: Cambridge University Press, 1984), and David Hammack, *Power and Society: Greater New York at the Turn of the Century* (New York: Russell Sage Foundation, 1982).

This new work is written in part in response to the so-called functional theory of the political machine, which was formulated by sociologist Robert K. Merton in *Social Theory and Social Structure* (New York: Free Press, 1949). Merton argued that machines gained and kept power, in spite of their manifest corruption, because of the "latent" functions they provided for society, which included the provision of jobs and social welfare services to immigrants and economic stability for business. Many portrayals of bosses and machines written in the 1950s and 1960s were influenced by this theory, including two classics: Oscar Handlin's *The Uprooted* (New York: Grosset and Dunlap, 1951) and Richard Hofstadter's *The Age of Reform* (New York: Vintage, 1955). John Allswang has written a history of reactions to the political machine from the perspective of the functional theory in *Bosses, Machines, and Urban Voters: An American Symbiosis* (Port Washington, N.Y.: Kennikat Press, 1977).

Authors writing within the functional framework thought they were correcting a moralistic criticism of the machines that dominated the literature around the turn of the twentieth century, but, as I argue in the Introduction, opinion on the machines in the time of Plunkitt varied from the hostility of James Bryce in *The American Commonwealth* (London: Macmillan, 1888) to the more ambivalent view of Lincoln Steffens in *The Shame of the Cities* (New York: McClure, Phillips and Co., 1904) or Jane Addams, whose article "Why the Ward Boss Rules" formed the core of a stirring last chapter in her book *Democracy and Social Ethics* (New York: Macmillan, 1902).

Changing opinions of the political machine can be followed in the introductions to previous editions of *Plunkitt of Tammany Hall* itself. Roy V. Peel's introduction to the 1948 edition (New York: Knopf) reflects the ambivalence of the Progressive era, questioning Plunkitt's importance and claims of generosity and attacking his dismissal of reformers. In his introduction to the 1963 edition (New York: E. P. Dutton), Arthur Mann reveals the influence of the functional theory, stressing Plunkitt's services to his constituents, although by no means approving of his graft.

The introductions to these previous editions, although based on little research into primary sources, are the only sustained analyses of either Plunkitt or Riordon, who are only briefly noted in the secondary works that mention them at all. I have noted the most important sources on their lives in the footnotes to my introduction. Two other useful analyses of the Tammany Democracy in the days of Plunkitt are Nancy Weiss, *Charles Francis Murphy, 1858–1924: Respectability and Responsibility in Tammany Politics* (Northhampton, Mass.: Smith College, 1968), and Robert Wesser, *A Response to Progressivism: The Democratic Party and New York Politics, 1902–1918* (New York: New York University Press, 1986). Christopher Wilson provides a useful context for understanding the work of journalists like Riordon and Steffens in *The Labor of Words: Literary Professionalism in the Progressive Era* (Athens, Ga.: University of Georgia Press, 1985).

Index